# PROCLAMATIO COMMENTARIES

- The Old Testament
  Witnesses for Preaching

Foster R. McCurley, *Editor*

# DEUTERONOMY, JEREMIAH

## Elizabeth Achtemeier

**FORTRESS PRESS**     Philadelphia, Pennsylvania

**Library of Congress Cataloging in Publication Data**

Achtemeier, Elizabeth Rice, 1926–
    Deuteronomy, Jeremiah.

    (Proclamation commentaries)
    Bibliography: p.
    Includes index.
    1. Bible. O. T. Deuteronomy—Commentaries.
    2. Bible. O. T. Jeremiah--Commentaries. I. Title.
    BS1275.3.A35      222'.15'06      77–15226
    ISBN 0-8006-0590-X

6512177    Printed in the United States of America    1-590

# CONTENTS

In memory of
James Muilenburg
who taught so many of us what
it means to be a member of the
new Israel in Christ.

# EDITOR'S FOREWORD

This present volume continues *Proclamation Commentaries–The Old Testament Witnesses for Preaching*. Like its New Testament counterpart, this series is not intended to replace traditional commentaries which analyze books of the Bible by pericope or verse by verse. This six-volume series attempts to provide background material on selected Old Testament books which, among other things, will assist the reader in using *Proclamation: Aids for Interpreting the Lessons of the Church Year*. Material offered in these volumes consists of theological themes from various witnesses or theologians out of Israel's believing community. It is our expectation that this approach—examining characteristic themes and motifs—will enable the modern interpreter to comprehend more clearly and fully a particular pericope which contains or alludes to such a subject. In order to give appropriate emphasis to such issues in the brief form of these volumes, the authors present the results, rather than the detailed arguments, of contemporary scholarship.

On the basis of its concern to address the specific tasks of preaching and teaching the Word of God to audiences today, this commentary series stresses the theological dilemmas which Old Testament Israel faced and to which her witnesses responded. Accordingly, the historical and political details of Israel's life and that of her ancient Near Eastern neighbors are left to other books. Selected for discussion here are those incidents and issues in Israel's history which have a direct relationship to the theological problems and responses in her existence. Since the Word of God is always addressed to specific and concrete situations in the life of people, the motifs and themes in these commentaries are directed to those selected situations which best exemplify a certain witness's theology.

This volume deals with the profound and complex witnesses in the books of Deuteronomy and Jeremiah. Why is it that a Pentateuchal book and a prophetic book appear in the same commentary of this series? The answer to that question can be quite simple: since the turn of the century, scholars have recognized many affinities in the language, style, and thought of these two books. The complexity of the answer, however, is all too obvious when one attempts to explain these affinities and thus the relationship of Jeremiah and Deuteronomy. Many scholars today date the writing of Deuteronomy as well as the prophet Jeremiah in the seventh century B.C. It is, moreover, assumed that the original Deuteronomy consisted of that scroll found by Josiah's men in the temple at Jerusalem in 621 B.C. The extent to which that scroll is related to Josiah's reform depends on whether one gives priority to 2 Kings 22—23 where the finding of the scroll precedes the reform or to 2 Chronicles 34 where the discovery of the book follows the reform. The prophet Jeremiah becomes entangled in this affair by the question of his support or rejection of the Josianic/Deuteronomic reform. Was he called to be a prophet before the discovery of the scroll, in favor with Josiah's activity, and thus silent when the reform was in full swing? Or did his call to be a prophet come only after Josiah's death, and was he opposed to the principles of the reform?

The debate on these issues has produced a wide range of possibilities. As early as 1901, Bernhard Duhm argued that the affinities in Jeremiah with Deuteronomy were due to secondary prose material added to the otherwise primary discourses in the form of poetry. In 1913 Sigmund Mowinckel argued that there existed in Jeremiah "a Deuteronomistic source" which consisted of fifteen passages similar to Deuteronomy in expressions and ideas. More than thirty years later Mowinckel modified his view by arguing, not for a separate source but for a circle of tradition within which some of Jeremiah's sayings were transmitted and reinterpreted according to Deuteronomistic ideas and stylistic forms. In his commentary on Jeremiah, John Bright regards the relationship as exaggerated and argues that the style in question is typical of scribes in the seventh and sixth centuries B.C. and thus that the affinities are due to general scribal training rather than to direct dependence of one on the other. Finally, to round out the picture, E. W. Nicholson in *Preaching to the Exiles* returns to the conclusion (although with arguments different from those of Duhm) that all of the prose material in Jeremiah is due to Deuteronomistic authorship.

In the present volume Elizabeth Achtemeier presents lucidly the reasons for some of the various positions offered on the relationship between the two books and goes on to argue her own position in a convincing manner. With a careful weaving of historical matters and theological concerns, Professor Achtemeier deals with these intricate questions not as ends in themselves but as aids in interpreting the witnesses of these two books for the purpose of preaching and teaching the Word of God to today's audience.

It is the theological task which lies at the heart of this study of Deuteronomy and Jeremiah. The nature of God as the Divine Warrior is seen as an important motif which is developed in the two books—both in terms of God's warfare against his opponents and also in his protecting presence with his commissioned servants. At the same time, God's activity and invitation precede in both books the response he expects from those people whom he called to be his own. It is the task of his servants Moses and Jeremiah to speak to the people on God's behalf, mediate for the people before the jealous God, and suffer for the sins of the disobedient nation.

Interwoven with these basic theological positions, the motifs of love, remembrance, trust, worship, law, judgment, and hope are developed by the author in ways that are not only consistent explicitly with New Testament concerns but are integral to Christian theology and particularly to the proclamation of the Word of God to contemporary issues. Dr. Achtemeier's skill in and approach to the homiletical task of preaching from the Old Testament can be seen in her recent book *The Old Testament and the Proclamation of the Gospel* (1973).

Elizabeth Achtemeier has been Visiting Professor of Homiletics at Union Theological Seminary in Virginia since 1973. She served in a similar capacity at Pittsburgh Theological Seminary in 1976–77; for fourteen years she was Visiting Lecturer in Old Testament at Lancaster Theological Seminary. Besides the volume mentioned above, she has co-authored several books with her husband Paul and has contributed to the *Interpreter's Dictionary of the Bible* (1962) as well as its recent supplementary volume (1976). In addition to her publications in the area of Old Testament studies, Professor Achtemeier has written books on the feminine crises in the Christian faith and on marriage.

Fall 1977                                          FOSTER R. MCCURLEY
                    Lutheran Theological Seminary at Philadelphia

## CHAPTER ONE

# INTRODUCING DEUTERONOMY

In the minds of many people, no book seems less likely to inspire great preaching or to nurture the life of the Christian church than Deuteronomy. In the first place, it appears so ancient. It is presented to us in the Bible as a collection of three long addresses by Moses (1:1—4:43; 4:44—28:68; 29:1—30:20) to Israel in the plain of Moab (1:5), shortly before Israel's entrance into the promised land of Canaan. It ends with four appendixes detailing the last acts of Moses (chap. 31), a song sung by him (chap. 32), his final blessing (chap. 33) and an account of his death (chap. 34).

Second, the book appears so irrelevant to Christian faith. Its very title means "repeated/second law," and though that designation comes from the Vulgate's mistaken rendering of "copy" in 17:18, it nevertheless indicates our feeling about the book: that it is law, legalism, dry statutes and testimonies and ordinances, having little relation to the life of the spirit and of justification by faith.

If we can cast aside our unschooled stereotypes of Deuteronomy and examine its actual nature, however, we will find that there is no book of more importance in the Old Testament, and no Old Testament book more basic for understanding the New Testament than Deuteronomy. It is one of the four Old Testament books most frequently quoted in the New Testament—eighty-three times altogether. It presents the basic biblical understandings of the nature of Yahweh, of his people, of his covenant, of the relationship of law and grace, of worship and of the ethical life. It not only states but fully expounds the first and greatest commandment. It can be said that Deuteronomy's message is an Old Testament foreshadowing of the New Testament gospel, and it is no accident that its words are often heard from the lips of our Lord (Matt. 4:4, 7, 10; 7:7; 17:17;

John 7:24; 8:35). It was the spirit of Deuteronomy's gracious law which Jesus Christ fulfilled, though scribes and Pharisees had turned its mercy into merciless legalism (Matt. 5:17–20). But to understand this, we must see Deuteronomy in its proper setting and actual form.

Deuteronomy purports to be the final speeches to Israel by Moses before his death, on the eastern side of the Jordan (cf. similar farewell speeches in Josh. 23 and 1 Sam. 12). As such, it would date from about 1250–1200 B.C., and there are a number of conservative scholars who have defended the Mosaic authorship of at least large portions of the book. On the other hand, some have dated it as late as the fifth century B.C., while a few put it in the tenth or eleventh century B.C.

Most persuasive have been those critics who have dated Deuteronomy in the seventh century B.C. Such a date became widely accepted after the work of de Wette, and it is now accepted by the majority of biblical scholars. It rests on several lines of argument: 1) Many of Deuteronomy's laws are already present in the (ninth century?) Book of the Covenant (Exod. 20:22—23:33), but Deuteronomy's version presupposes a more advanced stage of the community's life (cf. Exod. 23:10ff. with Deut. 15:1ff.). Yet Deuteronomy shows nothing of the influence of the exilic and post-exilic Holiness and Priestly Codes. Similarly, there is no trace of Deuteronomic language in the writings of the eighth century prophets, but that vocabulary and style permeate the Book of Jeremiah. 2) Deuteronomy presupposes the preaching of the eighth century prophets, especially Hosea. 3) Deuteronomy presents traditions about the forefathers and Moses which possess an almost canonical status, evidence of a long period of development and transmission. 4) The "book of the law" found during the repair of the temple in the eighteenth year (622/21) of King Josiah's reign in Judah (2 Kings 22—23) was some form of the Book of Deuteronomy. The measures carried out by Josiah, and especially the centralization of all worship in Jerusalem, are called for in no other book of the Old Testament. Some would say that the centralization laws are ambiguous, but few scholars doubt that the book played a leading role in the Josianic reform.

Deuteronomy's audience is therefore Judah in the seventh century B.C. The people stand in their imagination where thirteenth century B.C. Israel once stood—before Moses in the wilderness to hear his final words. Israel's former history is still present, but it is seventh century Israel's history too. They are there, making the long trek through the wilderness after the deliverance from Egypt. They stand at the foot of Mt. Horeb (Sinai) to enter into covenant with their God (cf. 5:3–4).

That which Moses delivers to Israel in Deuteronomy is the full revelation of Yahweh's will. The further conception of the book is that Israel received only the Ten Commandments at Mt. Horeb (5:6–27), but that Yahweh made known all his commandments to Moses at that time (5:31). Before his death, Moses therefore passed on to Israel the rest of Yahweh's words, and Deuteronomy is conceived as the content of that teaching (6:1).

It is by no means only law which Moses delivers to Israel in these final speeches. Deuteronomy does contain many statutes and ordinances. But it is law or *tôrāh* only in the Old Testament sense of the term: it is "teaching" or "instruction" in how to live as the people of God. As such, it deals with Israel's origin and the reason for her being, with her future and the fulfillment of her existence, with her attitude and her motivations for action. It is meant to be Yahweh's total revelation. It therefore states that it is not to be added to or taken from (4:2; 12:32), and Israel is not to turn aside from it either to the right hand or the left (5:32; cf. 17:20; 28:14).

In short, Deuteronomy claims for itself canonical status, and the fact that it is to be placed in the ark beside the tablets of the Decalogue emphasizes its authority (31:24–26). Even more important, the fact that for the first time, in the reform of Josiah, a written book becomes a standard by which people, prophets, priests, and kings are measured is a significant development in Israel's history which leads eventually to the process of the canonization of the written Scriptures as a whole.

We will understand correctly Deuteronomy and the meaning of canon only if we look more closely at the nature of its laws. There are found both types of law so familiar to us from the study of

Albrecht Alt: case laws (21:1ff., 15ff., 18ff., etc.) and apodictic or unconditional laws (5:7ff.; 15:1; 16:19, etc.). There are laws arranged into series (16:21—17:1; 23:2-8), and laws which deal with a subject in a series of exhortations (the prophets, 13:1-5; the king, 17:14-20; the Mosaic prophet, 18:15-22; note that all these point to a date in the time of the monarchy).

It is these exhortative laws which characterize Deuteronomy's tone. For example, if we examine 18:15-22, it is clear that it contains only two apodictic stipulations: verse 15, "him you shall heed"; verse 20, "But the prophet . . . who speaks in the name of other gods, that same prophet shall die." In the rest of the passage, there is promise (vv. 15, 18), historical retrospect (vv. 16f.), divine warning (vv. 19, 20a), instruction (vv. 21f.), comfort (v. 22d)— all characteristics much more of preaching than of legal prescription.

These characteristics are by no means confined to a few passages in Deuteronomy. In 15:1-11 concerning the year of release, for example, the basic apodictic command is given in verse 1, followed by its legal interpretation in verses 2-3. From that point on, we find promise and warning, exhortation and instruction. Or in regard to the laws concerning witnesses and the *lex talionis* in 19:15-21, a comparison with the parallel passages in Numbers 35:30, Exodus 21:23-25, and Leviticus 24:19f. makes it clear that the authors of Deuteronomy have gone to some length to explain the laws and to exhort the hearers to "hear, and fear, and . . . never again commit any such evil. . . ."

Such exhortation is not so prominent in some sections (cf. chaps. 22—25), a characteristic which is perhaps a sign of unredacted additions to the book. Nevertheless, Deuteronomy as a whole gives the impression far more of preaching and teaching than it does of legalistic prescription. This initial written canon is presented not in the form of legalistic command, but as an appeal to faith. Like that of the Bible as a whole, the canonical status of Deuteronomy rests not on automatic and unthinking obedience, but on understanding and heartfelt participation in a community of trust and experience.

Deuteronomy is aimed at the hearts and minds and wills of its hearers. That is its principal characteristic. It is preaching which confronts its audience personally and requires from them a personal response, out of the depths of hearts and understandings of minds and freedom of wills. There is no false appeal to authority of power or office, no moralistic demand to obey without thinking, no emotional reliance on crowd psychology. Some of the passages in the book are singular and are addressed to individuals; others are plural in the Hebrew (e.g., 5:1—6:1; 9:7b—10:11; 11:2–32; 12:1–12; 17:16–20). But in both cases, those addressed are bidden to respond to Yahweh from the depths of their being (cf. 4:29; 6:5; 11:13; 26:16; 30:2). The central message is summed up in 10:12–22, of which verse 12 reads:

> And now, Israel, what does the Lord your God require of you, but to fear the Lord your God, to walk in all his ways, to love him, to serve the Lord your God with all your heart and with all your soul.

The call of the book is, "Circumcise therefore the foreskin of your heart, and be no longer stubborn" (10:16; cf. 30:6, 10). When Israel knows God, she is to know him in her inward parts (4:39; 8:5). She is to listen and hear (5:1; 6:3f.; 27:9) and lay all his words on her heart (32:46).

Equally, Deuteronomy is concerned that Israel understand Yahweh's words. It calls also for a response of the mind, and no biblical book makes more effort to clarify the law and Yahweh's actions and the reasons for them. Everything is explained and simplified and made comprehensible to the laity. Nothing is treated which belongs to the esoteric realm of ritual and clergy and which therefore cannot be grasped by ordinary men and women and even children (a marvelous standard for preaching still today!). For example, 8:1–10 carefully explains why Israel is to obey the commandments (v. 1), and what Yahweh was doing with Israel in the wilderness (v. 2), and what he was teaching his people there (v. 3), and what the nature of his relationship with them was (v. 5), and what the future is that he has planned for them (vv. 7–10).

Moses characterizes his words in Deuteronomy as "teaching" (4:1, 5, 14; 5:31; 6:1; cf. 31:19, 22), and that which Israel has to do is "learn" (4:10; 5:1; 14:23; 17:19; 31:12f.). That is, Israel is to absorb Moses' teachings and thereby know Yahweh and his commandments within her inner self. What Israel inwardly learns will determine her actions (cf. 18:9), and her obedience rests upon her thorough understanding (cf. 32:7, 28f.), which is her uniqueness among the nations (4:6).

The adults in Israel, and especially fathers, are therefore to "teach" their children the ways and words of God. No biblical book lays more stress on the religious education of the young than does Deuteronomy (4:9f.; 6:7; 11:19; 31:13). Neither is there any thought that children and adults cannot absorb the words of *tôrāh* and thus be obedient (cf. 30:11–14).

Deuteronomy presents its call to faith through the instrument of the personal confrontation of preaching. Thus Israel is placed in the situation of immediate address and required to make a decision, and that decision is to involve her heart and mind and strength. Given the nature of its message, Deuteronomy probably could have taken no other form than that of preaching, because it is in that activity, above all others, that God confronts his people.

## CHAPTER TWO

# THE BACKGROUND OF DEUTERONOMY

## THE HISTORICAL SCENE

From the beginning of the reign of Tiglath-pileser III in 745 B.C. until the death of Ashurbanipal in 627 B.C., the Assyrian Empire once again dominated the ancient Middle East. Tiglath-pileser adopted the policy of conquering small states, deporting their populations, and turning their territory into Assyrian provinces. It was not a totally new measure, but it was applied by Tiglath-pileser and his successors (Shalmaneser V, Sargon II) with a new consistency, and the Assyrian might thus became the most feared and hated in the ancient world. The northern kingdom of Israel fell victim to it at the hands of Sargon II (722–705) in 722/21 B.C. and disappeared from history. The southern kingdom of Judah under Hezekiah (715–687/86) was spared only by the payment of an enormous tribute, the loss of much of her territory, and the impoverishment of her national life.

To be sure, Assyria had to face repeated threats from Egypt. But every Israelite and Judean attempt to rely on Egyptian aid during the period ended in disappointment (cf. Isa. 30:1–5; 31:1–3), and it is no surprise that Hezekiah's son, Manasseh (687/86–642) therefore was content to play faithful vassal to Assyria, first under Esarhaddon (681–669) and then Ashurbanipal. As sign of his subservience, Manasseh erected altars to the Assyrian astral deities in the temple (2 Kings 21:5) and gave sanction to divination and magic (v. 6).

Hezekiah had tried earlier to reform the religious life of Judah (2 Kings 18:4; cf. 2 Chron. 29—31). In fact, it was Hezekiah's bid to reclaim the northern territories and to reestablish the Davidic dynasty, centralized around worship in Jerusalem (2 Chron. 30:1–

12), which was partly responsible for his crushing defeat at the hands of Sennacherib in 701 B.C.

Manasseh therefore took exactly the opposite tack (2 Kings 21:3–16). He restored the local shrines throughout the countryside and gave free reign to foreign cults and practices of every kind. Foreign attire appeared in the royal court (Zeph. 1:8). Fertility rites and sacred prostitution were practiced even in the temple (cf. 2 Kings 23:4–7). The barbarous practice of human sacrifice again made its appearance (cf. Jer. 7:31). Prophets and Rechabites who protested (cf. Jer. 35) were put to death. Violence, fraud, and injustice became the accepted mode in government and commerce (cf. Zeph. 1:9, 3:3), with the inhabitants of Jerusalem cynically certain that Yahweh could do nothing about it (Zeph. 1:12).

But according to the prophets, Yahweh could do something about it. He could destroy Assyria (cf. Zeph. 2:13–15; Isa. 9:1; 10:12–19, 24–27; 33:1). And it was during the reign of Ashurbanipal that the giant empire began to totter. Shortly after 655 B.C. Psammetichus I (663–609) of Egypt, supported by King Gyges of Lydia, broke free from Assyrian domination and founded the Twenty-sixth Dynasty. Chaldean elements of the population in Babylonia, spurred on by Elam in the East, grew restless under the deputy rule of Ashurbanipal's older brother. Medes from western Iran and barbarian Cimmerians and Scythians from the Caucasus began to press against the northern frontier. In 652 B.C., Babylon was shaken by a general rebellion, Palestine and Syria stirred restlessly, and Arab tribes from the Syrian desert overran Edom and Moab. Ashurbanipal mastered the situation only with great difficulty.

In the meantime, Manasseh died and was replaced by his son Amon (642–640), but the latter was assassinated by what scholars now believe to have been an anti-Assyrian party in the Judean court (2 Kings 21:19–23). However, the time was not fully ripe for freedom. Free landholders ("people of the land," 2 Kings 21:24) executed the assassins and put the eight-year old Josiah, son of Amon, on the throne.

In the year that Josiah came of age (627/26 B.C.), Ashurbanipal died, to be followed by two weakling sons in succession. In October of 626 B.C., the Babylonians under the leadership of Prince Nabopolassar, defeated the Assyrians outside Babylon and set up an independent throne there which, try as they would, the Assyrians could not dislodge. At the same time, the Medes under Cyaxares, prepared for attack on Assyria.

Sensing his opportunity, Josiah of Judah made his move for independence. According to the account in 2 Chronicles 34, Josiah began measures to remove foreign influence not only from Judah and Jerusalem, but also from the northern territory "as far as Naphtali" (v. 6). Like Hezekiah before him, his purpose was to reestablish the borders of the Davidic Empire. He therefore not only purged the temple and Jerusalem and Judah of their foreign and pagan cults, suppressed the practice of magic and divination, and put to death the eunuch priests and sacred prostitutes of the fertility cults (2 Chron. 34:3–5; 2 Kings 23:4–14, 24), but he also destroyed the shrines of Samaria and put their priests to death (2 Kings 23:15–20).

Chronicles maintains that the Book of the Law was not found until *after* these widespread reforms, and that the only result of the find was a covenant ceremony for king and people, followed by a passover celebration (2 Chron. 34:29—35:19). The account in 2 Kings 22—23, on the other hand, attributes the whole of the reform to Josiah's reaction to the Book of the Law. Both accounts have been schematized, and the truth probably lies somewhere in between. The fact that the temple was undergoing repairs when the book was found indicates that reform measures had already begun, and Josiah undoubtedly began the elimination of Assyrian influences and the extension of his rule northward already in 626 B.C. The discovery of the book in 622/21 probably led to the second stage of the reform, when the Yahweh cult itself was thoroughly purified of pagan and especially baalistic, Canaanite influences. Local cult sites throughout the land were done away, and the rural priests were invited to come to Jerusalem.

Certainly Josiah's anguished reaction to the reading of the Book of the Law (2 Kings 22:11–13, 19; 2 Chron. 34:19, 27) was occasioned by a new realization of the corruption of the chosen people themselves, and the second stage of the reform was a thoroughgoing effort to make that people once more pleasing to their God. But there was a further measure in Deuteronomy which accounted for Josiah's strong reaction to the book. Deuteronomy contained a law of the king (Deut. 17:14–20), which made the authority of the monarch second to that of the Deuteronomic legislation.

It must never be forgotten that Josiah was a Davidic king, occupying a throne which had been guaranteed by God (2 Sam. 7). His palace was located next to the temple in which God himself dwelt, and both were on Mt. Zion, Yahweh's holy hill, which Isaiah had prophesied would never be captured (Isa. 10:27b–34; 29:1–8; 31:1–9; cf. Pss. 46, 48, 76; Mic. 4:11–13). There was therefore attached to the monarchy, in the popular mind, an absolute guarantee of the divine pleasure and blessing.

But then Josiah was confronted by the words of Deuteronomy, which proclaimed that his rule and the welfare of his kingdom were dependent on obedience to the Mosaic covenant demands of Deuteronomy, and which promised that a curse would fall on those who were disobedient. The promise to David was not an absolute guarantee of God's favor—for either king or people! That was the revelation from Deuteronomy which caused Josiah such anguished repentance, and the covenant into which Josiah entered placed him and his people under the authority of Mosaic law—the first time in which the Davidic covenant had been so subordinated (2 Kings 23:3).

## THE STRUCTURE OF THE BOOK

Certainly Deuteronomy is redacted as a covenant document. As early as 1938, Gerhard von Rad pointed out that Deuteronomy's structure is not an *ad hoc* creation, but reflects the form and content of a cultic festival, which also lies behind Exodus 19—24.

Further light was thrown on the form of the book when George E. Mendenhall pointed out the similarities between the covenant formulations of the Old Testament and Hittite suzerainty treaties of the late bronze age (1400–1200 B.C.). The latter had six basic elements, which are reflected in the Old Testament: 1) a preamble identifying the king offering the treaty (cf. Deut. 1:1–5; Exod. 20:1–2; Josh. 24:2); 2) a historical recital of the past relations between the suzerain and his vassal, emphasizing the deeds of kindness done by the sovereign for the dependent state (cf. Deut. 5—11; Josh. 24:3–13); 3) the covenant stipulations, which demanded exclusive loyalty to the suzerain (cf. Deut. 12—26; Exod. 20:3—23:19); 4) provision for the deposit of the treaty in the sanctuary and for periodic public reading of the law (cf. Deut. 10:1–5; 31:10–13); 5) the invocation of deities as witnesses to the treaty (cf. Deut. 4:26; 30:19; 31:28; Josh. 24:22, 26f.); 6) a series of blessings and curses on those who kept or violated the treaty obligations (cf. Deut. 27:15—28:68; Exod. 23:20f.; Lev. 26:3ff.).

This relationship of Deuteronomy to ancient Near Eastern covenant forms has been further investigated by Meredith G. Kline, Dennis J. McCarthy, Gordon J. Wenham, and Moshe Weinfeld. The latter holds that Deuteronomy is a literary creation of scribes and wise men of the eighth and seventh centuries B.C., who took the motifs of an old covenant tradition and reworked them into a literary covenant pattern, closely parallel to Assyrian treaties of the time. It is doubtful that Deuteronomy's urgent preaching is the result of scribal formulations, but it is almost beyond question that the structure of Deuteronomy is related in some way to the structure of ancient Near Eastern political treaties and that the form of the book represents a carefully redacted document.

It is also almost beyond question that the entire present Book of Deuteronomy was not discovered in the temple in the time of Josiah. The book itself gives evidence of repeated additions to it: 1) there are several titles (1:1; 4:44; 6:1; 12:1), and some scholars have found at least two conclusions; 2) the form of address alternates between singular and plural; 3) there are repetitions and obviously later additions within the work. Although some scholars have defended the unity of the book, it is almost universally accepted that the present Deuteronomy is the final product of a long and complex process of growth.

Martin Noth made one of the most significant contributions to research on Deuteronomy when he pointed out that chapters 1—3(4) and parts of chapters 31 and 34 did not originally belong to Deuteronomy at all, but were added to the book when it was incorporated into the larger Deuteronomic History (Deut.—2 Kings) about 550 B.C. Deuteronomy 4:44—30:20 was originally a complete book in itself, although the plural passages in it were somewhat later than the singular.

With some modifications Noth's views have been widely accepted. Many scholars have concluded that the original Deuteronomy contained most of chapters 5—26 and much of 28, with 4:44 and following forming the introduction to it. Certainly the corpus of 4:44—30:20 was formed very early in the history of the book's growth, and for our purposes can be regarded as a whole.

## THE HOME OF DEUTERONOMY

Certainly prominent in the book is an interest in the cultic traditions of the old Israelite tribal federation. One of the features of that federation or amphictyony was the "Holy War," a phenomenon first fully illumined by von Rad. Von Rad showed that the wars of Israel in the time of the judges and through the reign of Saul were conducted according to specific cultic rules by the free farmers of the land, who voluntarily gathered behind a charismatic leader to fight against an attacking foe. The concept of the Holy War, moreover, was that Yahweh was the chief warrior, fighting on behalf of the hosts of Israel. It is this concept which permeates Deuteronomy. Not only does it contain many laws taken from the language and customs of the Holy War (20:1–20; 21:10–14; 23:9–14; 24:5; 25:17–19), but its speeches are also saturated with the ideology of the Holy War (6:18f; 7:1ff.; 7:16–26; 12:29f.; 19:1f.).

Again, Deuteronomy preserves the tribal federation's negative attitude toward the kingship. Because the Israelite amphictyony was a theocracy, it had no place for a king (cf. Judg. 8:22ff.; 9:7ff.; 1 Sam. 8:7), and although Deuteronomy was written in the time of the monarchy and had to make room for the kingship, it does so only by subordinating the monarch to the covenant law and placing him on a level with every other Israelite.

It therefore seems clear that the original home of Deuteronomy was the northern kingdom of Israel. It was there that the tribal federation had its center, first at Shechem (Josh. 8:33; 24:1), perhaps for a short time at Gilgal (Josh. 4:19; 5:9; 9:6) and Bethel (Judg. 20:18, 26–28; 21:2), and finally for the longest time at Shiloh (Josh. 18:1; Judg. 18:31; 1 Sam. 1:3, 24; 3:3; Jer. 7:12, 14). It was at the amphictyonic center that the festival of covenant renewal was celebrated annually (Judg. 21:19; 1 Sam 1:3), and it has been maintained that even after the amphictyony was broken up by the Philistines, the old covenant traditions were preserved at these sanctuaries (see Nicholson).

In addition, there are many affinities between Deuteronomy and the Book of the Covenant (see von Rad, *IDB*), as well as between Deuteronomy and the E source of the Pentateuch (see Wright, *IB*), and both the Book of the Covenant and E are regarded as of northern origin. Also, Deuteronomy shares some style and content with Hosea, the only northern prophet to have his preaching collected into a book. Deuteronomy's struggle against syncretism fits much better in the North, and it is addressed to all Israel, a concept which had its home in the North.

It has also been argued that the most important special feature of Deuteronomy—the centralization of the cult (12:5, 11, 14, 18, 21, 26; 14:23–25; 15:20; 16:2, 6f., 11, 15f; 17:8; 26:2; 31:11)—was modeled after the central shrine of the amphictyony. In the tribal federation, the central cult object was the ark, conceived as the base for the throne of the invisible Yahweh, who was enthroned above the cherubim (cf. 1 Sam. 4:4). But Deuteronomy has several important differences from this amphictyonic concept. Yahweh is not enthroned at the central sanctuary, but lives in heaven (Deut. 4:36; 26:15); he allows only his name to dwell at the chosen sanctuary. The ark is merely a container for the law, not the base of Yahweh's throne (10:1–5; 31:9, 24–26). Sacrifices, firstlings, and tithes are now offered only at the central sanctuary (contrary to amphictyonic practice), and Passover, originally a family festival, is turned into a pilgrimage to the central sanctuary.

Some scholars who connect Deuteronomy's centralization law with amphictyonic traditions maintain that the "name theology" ("the place where I cause my name to dwell") represented in Deuteronomy arose in the North. But it is more probable that the "name theology" was a unique contribution of Deuteronomy itself.

Others have argued that there really is no law of centralization in Deuteronomy and that "the place which the Lord your God shall choose" could refer to a number of authorized sanctuaries, but such views have found little support. It is our position that the centralization of the cult was a central feature of Deuteronomy from the beginning. Whether that centralization was patterned after the old Israelite federation's worship at a central shrine remains problematic however.

Nevertheless, Deuteronomy's original home was northern Israel, and we therefore have to ask who it was in the North who formulated Deuteronomy's sermons. Several possibilities have been suggested: 1) a reform group which arose after 722/21 (Alt); but Deuteronomy ill-fits the devastated northern situation; 2) a revival movement before 722/21, which emphasized Bethel as the central shrine (Dumermuth); 3) a group of northern Levites, expelled by Jeroboam I from Bethel and Dan (cf. 1 Kings 12:31f.) and centered at Shechem, who also influenced Hosea (Wolff); but there is no evidence in Hosea of such a group and Shechem is condemned in that book (Hos. 6:9f.). Most important, it must also be explained how Deuteronomy then came to be found in the temple in the South.

Some scholars have argued that it was composed in the South in the first place (Rowley, Lohfink, Bächli), but the affinities of the book with the northern and amphictyonic traditions are too many to be denied.

Von Rad has, in a sense, straddled the question of whether Deuteronomy originated in the North or the South, by pointing to Shechem or Bethel in 722–622 B.C. as its place of origin, but he is understandably unwilling to say what form the book had during that century. It may have been a book of laws without sermons at that time. Von Rad is certain that the book found in the time of Josiah was the product of the preaching and redactive work carried on by priestly Levites throughout the Judean countryside. Only priests, argues von Rad, could have had Deuteronomy's knowledge of the old amphictyonic cultic and legal traditions, and yet reinterpreted them in so free a manner in Deuteronomy's paraenetic sections (cf. Neh. 8:7f.; 2 Chron 35:3). In addition, he believes that the Levites were the spokesmen of a free peasant movement for national independence in Judah after 701 B.C. In that year, Judah's regular mercenary army was destroyed by Sennacherib.

Thus the kingdom was forced to return to the traditions of the Holy War, with its volunteer army, and this accounts for the Holy War traditions in Deuteronomy.

Objections have been raised to von Rad's views: 1) Why would the country Levites centralize all worship in Jerusalem and thus abolish their own sanctuaries? Von Rad's reply is that not all parts of Deuteronomy know, or even assume, the centralization of the cult, and the centralization laws are somewhat later than the original work. Yet certainly the law of one cult site is an integral part of the theology of the book as a whole. 2) There is no evidence that the "people of the land" wanted any sort of reform in Judah. According to Jeremiah, they were as corrupt as everyone else (Jer. 34:17ff.; 37:2; 44:21ff.; cf. 5:1–9). 3) Von Rad offers no explanation of how the Book of the Law came to be hidden in the temple.

The other major theory concerning the authorship of Deuteronomy holds that its traditions stem from a prophetic party of the North, which fled to the South after 722/21 B.C. (Nicholson, et al.). There such prophets drew up a program of reform and revival with Jerusalem as the political and cultic center. That is, the prophetic reformers made concessions to the royal Zion traditions in order that the reform could be enforced by the Judean authorities. But they applied a term used previously only of David's election (*bāḥar*) to the election of Israel instead; they emphasized Yahweh's gift of the whole land rather than merely the gift of Zion; they substituted the "name theology" for the dwelling of Yahweh on Zion; they reinterpreted the significance of the ark.

The desire of the prophetic party was not just to reform the Jerusalem cult tradition, but to ensure the survival of Israel as a people. The reform of Hezekiah in 705 B.C. had been shortlived. Under Manasseh, apostasy once more spread throughout the land and the prophets were persecuted. It was among such persecuted prophets that the authors of Deuteronomy are to be found. The book was formulated during Manasseh's reign and then placed in the temple, where it was rediscovered in the time of Josiah. The reform had already begun under Josiah, but Deuteronomy added force to it. Deuteronomy was the product of a prophetic party, with ultimate roots in the North, who held the life and death aim of preserving what was left of Judah by restoring it to a genuine Mosaic faith over against apostasy and syncretism, corruption of the cult, and a pagan monarchy.

In support of this theory of the prophetic authorship of Deuteronomy, it has been pointed out that it is the only law code in the Old Testament which legislates concerning the prophets. It gives two tests of true prophecy (13:1–5; 18:21f.), and Moses, the covenant mediator, is understood as a prophet, not as a priest. Indeed, he is the model of all true prophets.

On the other hand, in support of von Rad's thesis, there is no doubt that the Levites are given a prominent place in Deuteronomy and are regarded as the true priests (18:1–8 et passim). It is they who are to have custody of the *tôrāh* (17:18; 31:9, 24ff.). Those who live outside of Jerusalem are to be allowed to come to Jerusalem and to minister in the temple, but 2 Kings 23:9 reflects the opposition of the Jerusalem Zadokite priesthood to this move. The result was that many Levites continued to live in the countryside, though deprived of their sanctuaries, and Deuteronomy directs that charity be given to them as to the widows and orphans (Deut. 12:19; 14:27–29; 16:11, 14; 26:12f.).

It therefore is difficult to say with certainty whether Deuteronomy is finally the product of prophets or of priests. Both groups preached and taught. Both were responsible for passing on the *tôrāh* in Israel. Both could have had intimate knowledge of the cultic and amphictyonic traditions, stemming ultimately from the North. In distinction from von Rad's views, there is no reason why prophets could not have been intimately connected with the cult, or why they could not have dealt with the cultic traditions with great freedom in their preaching: we have writing prophets in the Old Testament who give evidence of both characteristics. In addition, Jeremiah's close connection with Deuteronomy must be taken into account, as we shall see subsequently. But thus far in our discussion, there is no reason why both country Levites and prophets could not have contributed to the book, as members of a reform movement. We shall return to these matters in the discussion of the Book of Jeremiah.

## CHAPTER THREE

# THE WITNESS TO GOD

How do you reform and renew a people's religious life? That was a life and death question for the authors of Deuteronomy, because Israel could have no existence apart from her God. Like the Christian church, she was not a natural people, bound together by the ties of blood or race or soil. A conglomerate of semitic semi-nomadic tribes and families, she had been a mixed multitude when her God redeemed her from Egyptian captivity (cf. Exod. 12: 38); she was bound together as a people only by the memory of that common redemption and by her covenant relation with her one Redeemer, to whom she had freely pledged her sole loyalty (Exod. 24:3-8). When she forgot her God and his covenant, she therefore ceased to be a people (cf. Hos. 1:9; 1 Pet. 2:10), a fact which was demonstrated when the ten northern tribes of Israel disappeared from history. The authors of Deuteronomy were therefore literally fighting for Judah's life, seeking to recall her to loyalty to her God which would prevent her annihilation.

But Judah no longer even knew who God was. His nature had become confused with that of the Canaanite baals and of the Assyrian astral deities. Worshipers sought him in the processes of nature and in the movement of the stars, or they equated his will with the nostrums of popular prophets or with the pronouncements of the government. Over against such syncretism and blindness and corruption, the authors of Deuteronomy set their witness to God; the result was a proclamation fully consonant with the Christian gospel.

God, proclaimed the authors of Deuteronomy, makes known his nature to us by the deeds he has done in our lives. He is not found by a mystical escape to a spiritual realm, and he is not known as he is in himself (ontologically), but only as he has entered into a relationship with us and dealt with the concrete circumstances of our lives. His name is "Yahweh," which means "he who is indeed with you" (cf. Deut. 31:23; Exod. 3:13–15), and his dealings are personal, concrete, active, always effective of a change in our situation.

His revelation of himself does not take place through the created round of nature, because he is the Creator of heaven and earth, above and beyond all he has made (Deut. 10:14). Indeed, the picture of God which Deuteronomy draws deliberately contrasts with that of the Canaanite baals. Unlike them, Yahweh is not found as a diffused spirit and at countless local sanctuaries. Yahweh is one (6:4), to be worshiped at one sanctuary where he has put his name, by one united Israel, who pledges herself to obey one comprehensive tôrāh (Deuteronomy itself). At no other time in Israel's history is there such an emphasis on the unity of Yahweh's revelation of himself, and on the unity of the people to whom it is given. Yahweh, the one Lord, confronts Israel, the one people, past, present, and future (cf. 29:10–15). Just as in the New Testament, his person meets the church in one Lord, and there is one body and one Spirit, one hope, one faith, one baptism (Eph. 4:4–5). The revelation of God in the Bible is concrete, personal, defined.

The people of God know the nature of the Lord who confronts them by his actions in their lives. Thus the New Testament tells the story of the life, death and resurrection of Jesus Christ, and in similar fashion, Deuteronomy recites the sacred history with Yahweh. It tells how Yahweh brought Israel "forth out of the iron furnace, out of Egypt" (4:20) "by signs, by wonders, and by war, by a mighty hand and an outstretched arm, and by great terrors" (4:34; cf. 6:21–23; 7:8; 8:14). It relates how Israel stood at the foot of Mt. Horeb, "while the mountain burned with fire to the heart of heaven, wrapped in darkness, cloud, and gloom," and how Israel heard the voice of Yahweh from the fire, but saw no form of the invisible God, as she received the covenant commandments (4:11–13) and trembled with fear before God's glory and his greatness (5:22–27). It tells how Israel immediately rebelled against her covenant Lord by making the golden calf and how she was saved only by Moses' intercession (9:8–21). It recalls Israel's repeated lack of faith in the wilderness and her refusal to enter the promised land, and thus God's judgment on his people in the midst of his constant fatherly care for them (1:19–46).

The wilderness was a foreboding place, "great and terrible," with "fiery serpents and scorpions and thirsty ground where there was no water," but Yahweh fed his adopted sons and daughters (8:3, 5; 14:1; 32:19–20). He was their father (32:6, 18), who encircled them and cared for them, and kept them "as the apple of his eye" (32:10). He went before them in a cloud by day and in fire by night, even showing them where to pitch their tents (1:31–33). He fed them with manna and gave them water to drink out of the rock, that they might learn to depend on him for their life (8:3, 16). He kept their clothing from wearing out and their feet from going unshod (8:4; 29:5). For forty years he accompanied them, and because he was there, they lacked no necessity (2:7).

More than this, Yahweh was the warrior-conqueror for Israel. He battled for her against Sihon and Og and gave their land to the tribes of Reuben and Gad and the half-tribe of Manasseh (2:26–3:17).

It is in all these acts that Israel has learned who her God is. To her, all these things have been shown "that you might know that the Lord is God; there is no other besides him" (4:35). She is to "know therefore this day, and lay it to . . . heart, that the Lord is God in heaven above and on the earth beneath; there is no other" (4:39). It is on the basis of these deeds of power wrought by God in her history that Israel is to confess her faith: "He is your praise; he is your God, who has done for you these great and terrible things which your eyes have seen" (10:21).

There is also great emphasis placed on the love which this great and terrible God astoundingly has had for his people. God has been Israel's "redeemer" in the exodus (7:8; 9:26; 15:15; 24:18; cf. 21:8), taking the part of the kinsman to buy back his son out of slavery (cf. Exod. 4:22–23; Lev. 25:47ff.), Yahweh has "saved" Israel, that is, he has brought those under restraint into a broad place (33:29; cf. 32:15). But the final wonder for the Deuteronomists is the long process of preparation Yahweh has gone through to make a people for himself. Far back in the distant past, he set his love on the fathers and chose them and their descendants after them (4:37; 10:15), and the reason for the choice was simply that he might bestow his abundant life upon them.

In contrast to the Yahwist's epic (cf. Gen. 12:3), Deuteronomy says nothing about Israel's relation to the rest of the world in the purpose of God. Israel is Yahweh's "holy people," to be sure, "a people for his own possession, out of all the peoples that are on the face of the earth" (Deut. 7:6; 14:2). In fact, only in Deuteronomy do we find the concept of a "holy people," rather than that of a "holy nation" (Exod. 19:6). The biblical concept of "holiness" means that Israel has been set apart to Yahweh for his special purpose and is therefore unlike any other people (Deut. 4:32–34). But there is nothing here which would indicate that Israel's salvation is to be a "witness" to the rest of the world, as in Isaiah 43:10, 12; 44:8, or that she is to be a blessing in the midst of the earth, as in Genesis 12:3 or Isaiah 19:24–25. The authors of Deuteronomy are concerned primarily with the proclamation of the astounding and abundant love of God, by which they wish to awaken in Israel's heart an answering and commensurate love. They therefore proclaim God's purpose to be simply that of bestowing upon his people abundant life.

Everywhere in Deuteronomy, such abundant life is understood in terms of the gift of the land. Certainly this is due partly to Deuteronomy's polemic against the worship of the Canaanite baals. But salvation is very concrete in Deuteronomy: it is synonymous with a prosperous and peaceful life in that land which Yahweh promised already to the fathers. In contrast to the other Hexateuchal sources, Deuteronomy understands the promise to the patriarchs and their descendants primarily in terms of the promise of the land (1:8, 35; 6:10, 23; 9:5; 10:11; 11:9, 21; 19:8; 26:3; 28:11; 30:20; 31:20; but see 1:10f.; 6:3; 10:22 for the promise of descendants). The blessings which Yahweh wishes to shower upon his people are therefore of this world and largely material (12:7; 15:6, 14; 16:10; 28:2ff.). In other Hexateuchal sources, the land is the inheritance of the tribe or clan; in Deuteronomy (and the Deuteronomic history), it is the inheritance of Israel as a whole. It is THE good, described as a single whole, which a loving God wishes to bestow on his elected people.

The goodness of the land is emphasized in its description in Deuteronomy. As in the earlier sources, it is a land "flowing with milk and honey" (6:3; 11:9; 26:9; 27:3; 31:20), but no other Old Testament writing matches the Eden-like quality ascribed to the land by the writers of Deuteronomy. It is specifically contrasted with the land of Egypt, where irrigation was necessary (11:10), and its abundance of rain is ascribed to the fact that Yahweh cares for it and never takes his eyes off it (11:11–12). By implication, it is contrasted with the "thirsty ground" which Israel trod in the wilderness (8:15; cf. v. 7). Above all, it is a place of "good," which is a *terminus technicus* in Deuteronomy, and its "good" consists in the fact that it will furnish, to overflowing measure, all of Israel's necessities (8:7–10).

Integral to the "goodness" of the land is also the concept of "rest" (3:20; 25:19). When Israel crosses over the Jordan into the land which Yahweh has promised her fathers, then she shall have "rest" from all of her enemies round about, so that she lives in safety (12:9–10; cf. Mic. 4:4).

It is Yahweh alone who will give this "good" of the land and its "rest." Yahweh is the owner of the land, a fact which is repeatedly the presupposition of Israel's sacrificial rites. Therefore Israel never owns the land for herself; she must be given it and hold it under conditions which we will examine in the next chapter. There is, in short, no mystical or naturalistic bond between Israel and the land. All mythological understandings of a "oneness" with nature fall before Israel's understanding of the land as a historical gift from God.

The promise of Israel's loving Lord is that she must not fear or be dismayed before the present inhabitants of the land when she enters in to take it, for just as Yahweh fought for her in the exodus and wilderness wanderings, so too he will fight for her in the conquest, driving out her enemies before her (7:17–24; 20:1–4; 31:3–8). Yahweh is the Divine Warrior in Deuteronomy (cf. 23:14), the leader of the amphictyonic hosts, who will not fail or forsake his people until he gives them victory.

Such views might be considered nothing more than the nationalistic rationalizations of a homeless people were it not for the fact that Deuteronomy emphasizes that Israel does not deserve the gift of the land. Israel's rebellion against her God is repeatedly recalled in Deuteronomy's historical recital (cf. 9:6ff.; 32:5f.). Thus Moses emphasizes to the people that it is not because of their righteousness that Yahweh will give them the land, but because of the wickedness of the Canaanite inhabitants, and above all, because Yahweh is a faithful God who will keep his promise to the fathers (9:4–5). Beyond all else, it is that promise embodying the electing love of God which fashions history in Deuteronomy's understanding and moves it toward its goal. For the sake of his promise, Yahweh forgives (9:27; 10:11). For the sake of his promise, he makes Israel his own (7:8).

But why the promise? Why did Yahweh set his love upon the fathers and choose them and their descendants after them? That is the question which Israel, in Deuteronomy and indeed the Bible as a whole, never can fully answer. Like every Christian who knows he is not worthy of the grace of God, Israel stands before the mystery of her election and can only say it was simply a gift out of the love of God. The ruler of the universe desires that we have abundant life. God loves us, while we are yet sinners, and leads us toward his fulfillment (Rom. 5:8–11).

It is in this sense that the Christian preacher can appropriate Deuteronomy's message concerning the promised land. The gift of the land is THE prominent good for Israel in Deuteronomy, and because that is so, the book often seems totally irrelevant to our theology and life. We have no theology of the land as such in the Christian proclamation. We do, however, have a theology of promise and fulfillment, and it is precisely in that context that the Epistle to the Hebrews picks up Deuteronomy's motif of the land with its "rest," and applies them to Christ (Heb. 3:7—4:13). In that epistle, Christ becomes the promised place of "rest." He is our "promised land." In short, Deuteronomy's concept of the land is understood in terms of the incarnation, as is true with so many other motifs of the Old Testament in the New (cf. the covenant, the temple, the sacrifice, the manna). Like Israel, we move toward the final good, the place of fulfillment, the promised abundant life. Despite our sin and constant rebellion, God sets his love upon us in Christ, as he set his love upon Israel, and now, with Paul, we strain "forward to what lies ahead." We "press on toward the goal for the prize of the upward call of God in Christ Jesus" (Phil. 3:13–14).

The future nature of the fulfillment becomes even clearer if we remember that Deuteronomy is actually addressed to the sinful people of Judah of the seventh century B.C.—a people who already live in the land, indeed a people whose ten northern tribes have already lost their land! Such facts make it clear that the land in Deuteronomy is really a unique combination of concrete present and ideal future qualities. Israel has quite concrete actions which she must do in the land in order to live upon it, as we shall see in the next chapters. But it is also always her future goal, the final fulfillment which God in his love wishes to bestow upon her. Israel is a people under way in Deuteronomy, as the church is always under way. She is a people who continually sins, and yet who, by the mercy of God, finds her sin expunged and herself set back once more at the time of her first election. The promise is held out to her that she can inherit abundant life in the land.

"*This day* you have become the people of the Lord your God" (Deut. 27:9): that is the gracious word which sinful Israel of the seventh century B.C. hears from Deuteronomy—that she is still God's covenant people—just as the church hears in the message of the cross, that she is still Christ's people despite her repeated sin. This God of the Bible loves us—for totally unfathomable reasons. He is a God who wills to be near at hand (Deut. 4:7), who enters into covenant fellowship with us, and who bids us make that real fellowship the basis of our faith and practice. If we do so, then the promise of Deuteronomy, and of the New Testament, is that we shall have abundant life in the place of fulfillment toward which we move in our pilgrimage.

## CHAPTER FOUR

# THE RESPONSE OF ISRAEL

There is no "cheap grace" in the Bible. Deuteronomy, like the rest of the Scriptures, proclaims the love and mercy of God, the actions by which he has redeemed and chosen and guided Israel, and the goal of abundant life in the land which he holds out as the final fulfillment to her. But at the same time, Deuteronomy repeatedly admonishes Israel that she must respond to the love of God and appropriate it for herself. God's grace and Israel's election are not automatic guarantees of Israel's life. She must grasp that grace and live out that election, or she will die.

This understanding of Israel's responsibility is spelled out in relation to the gift of the land. It is stated over and over again that Yahweh *gives* Israel the land, but she must also *possess* it (1:39; 3:18; 4:1; 5:31; 12:1; 15:4; 19:2, 14; 25:19); Yahweh brings Israel into the land, but she must also come into it; he gives over her enemies into her hand, but she must also smite them (see Miller). God acts, but Israel must also act in response; she must appropriate the salvation which Yahweh offers to her, just as the Christian must appropriate the salvation offered in Jesus Christ.

The land is further understood as the sphere where Israel is to make her response to Yahweh (4:14), and that response is spelled out in concrete terms of life in the land. In short, what Israel does in the place where she lives, in her historical, everyday existence, is the crucial test of her faith. She appropriates her salvation not by some mystical escape out of history, but by her actions within her specific, historical situation. Throughout Deuteronomy and the Deuteronomic history, the land is the place of testing for Israel, the place where she decides whether or not she will make Yahweh's gift of life and salvation her own.

The first response required of Israel in Deuteronomy is therefore the response of *trust* in Yahweh's purposes for her. Looking back at the long history by which Yahweh has made her his own and guided her to the land, Israel's response must be a basic belief that Yahweh in fact wants abundant life for her and is working in her life to achieve that goal. She must trust that Yahweh desires only good for her and not evil. Israel's attitude in the wilderness is specifically contrasted with such trust:

> . . . you murmured in your tents, and said, "Because the Lord hated us he has brought us forth out of the land of Egypt, to give us into the hand of the Amorites, to destroy us. Whither are we going up (Deut. 1:27-28a)?

The repeated answer of Deuteronomy's preachers to this doubting question about where they are going is the assurance that Yahweh is moving them toward life, concretized in the abundant goodness of the land. Israel must believe that. She must trust Yahweh's love.

Further, Israel must trust that Yahweh has the power to put his love into action, that he can indeed destroy her enemies before her (2:25; 7:17–21; 11:25), and that he will not fail or forsake her (31:6, 8, 23) until he has given her abundant life and rest in the promised land. Israel is to trust Yahweh's power to such an extent that she has no fear before her enemies (1:21, 29; 3:22; 7:18, 21; 20:3), because she knows that Yahweh is in her midst, fighting on her behalf (1:30; 7:21; 9:3; 20:4; 31:3, 6): "It is the Lord who goes before you; he will be with you, he will not fail you or forsake you; do not fear or be dismayed" (31:8).

Judah's trust is to rest very firmly on the memory of what Yahweh has done in her past, and the second response required of her throughout Deuteronomy is that she *remember*. She is to remember her slavery in Egypt (16:12; 24:22), and her deliverance in the exodus (5:15; 7:18; 15:15; 16:3; 24:18; cf. 6:12; 8:14). She is to remember the covenant at Horeb (cf. 4:9, 23) and her experiences in the wilderness (8:2; 9:7; 24:9; cf. 8:14 16). She is to remember all "the days of old" (32:7) and what Yahweh did in them, and thus she will be able to trust Yahweh's love and power in the present and future.

"To remember" in Deuteronomy is much more than simply recalling past history. It is so to live into that history that its events become contemporary and efficacious in the present, and that happens in Israel's cult. The constant emphasis in Deuteronomy is on "this day" (1:39; 2:18, 25, 30; 4:20, 38; 5:1, 3; 6:6, 24; 7:11; 8:11, 18; 9:1; 10:15; 11:2, 4, 28, 32; 12:8, etc.). The past becomes the present in Israel's worship of her God. Thus the third response required of her is *worship* "before the Lord."

There is no doubt that Deuteronomy emphasizes the reality of Yahweh's presence in the cult. The fact that Israel carries out her worship "before the Lord" occurs over twenty-five times (12:7, 12, 18; 14:26; 15:20; 16:11; 26:5, 10; 27:7; 29:10; 31:11, etc.), and the reason Israel can have fellowship with Yahweh is because he has chosen the central sanctuary and has put his "name" there (12:5, 11, 21; 14:23f.; 16:2, 6, 11). Apparently the "name" is not a fully hypostasized form of Yahweh, but nevertheless it represents for Deuteronomy his real fellowship with his people, and at the same time, his sovereign demand that Israel worship in the place he chooses.

Three yearly festivals are enjoined upon Israel in Deuteronomy 16: Passover and Unleavened Bread, Weeks, and Booths or Tabernacles. It is clearly stated that the purpose of Passover is that Israel may "remember" the day when she came out of Egypt (v. 3; cf. v. 12). Weeks was first a service of thanksgiving for the gift of the land (cf. v. 10), later a commemoration of the giving of the law on Horeb. In Deuteronomy 31:10–13, it is commanded that the whole of Deuteronomy be read at the Feast of Tabernacles in the ceremony of covenant renewal. Israel thus hears once again of Yahweh's guidance of her in history since the time of the fathers.

Similarly, at the ceremony of the offering of first-fruits, it is the historical recital of Yahweh's deeds which is the center of the worship rite. As the individual worshiper confesses what Yahweh has done, those past events become contemporaneous for him:

> A wandering Aramean was my father; and *he* went down into Egypt and sojourned there . . . And the Egyptians treated *us* harshly . . . Then *we* cried to the Lord . . . and the Lord brought *us* out of Egypt . . . And behold, now *I* bring the first of the fruit of the ground which thou, O Lord, hast given *me* (26:5–10).

Noth thinks perhaps there was even sacred drama in Israel's cult, when the sacred history was acted out. In any case, in Israel, as in the church, the worshiper reaches communion with God through the medium of a history which carefully and concretely defines the character of God.

The central response which is required of Israel in Deuteronomy to the God whom she meets in her history through the cult is the response of love. The term used is not *ḥesed*, covenant love, but *'āhab,* suggestive of the intense, interior, personal love of one family member for another (see Toombs). It has been pointed out (see Moran) that the ancient Near Eastern treaties required the vassal to manifest "love" toward the suzerain, but Deuteronomy goes far beyond this understanding. Further, in its constant polemic against Canaanite worship, Deuteronomy abandons Hosea's use of the marital relationship to picture the love between Yahweh and his people, and uses instead the analogy of the father-son relationship (Deut. 8:5; 14:1; cf. Hos. 11:1; Jer. 31:20). Israel is called to love Yahweh with the love of a son for his father. Thus Israel's love is to be a devotion which flows spontaneously and freely from the heart, in gratitude and response to Yahweh's fatherly love. Heartfelt love is the center of the covenant relation in Deuteronomy—Yahweh's love for Israel and Israel's answering love—and Israel is called at least twelve times in the book to manifest such love (5:10; 6:5; 7:9; 10:12; 11:1, 13, 22; 13:3; 19:9; 30:16, 20).

Certainly the primary text in this regard is the *šᵉmaʻ* ("Hear") in Deuteronomy 6:4–9, from which Jesus takes the first and greatest commandment (Mark 12:28–34 and pars.). The *šᵉmaʻ*, along with Deuteronomy 11:13–21 and Numbers 15:37–41, is still recited as a daily prayer by the Jews. Verse 5 in the passage is similar to Deuteronomy 10:12, and verses 5–9 are similar to 11:18–21. And all of these texts, as well as 13:3, call for love from the Israelite out of his whole undivided heart (i.e., mind) and soul (i.e., desire)— "with all your heart and with all your soul" is a favorite phrase in Deuteronomy (26:16; 30:2, 6, 10; cf. Jer. 32:41). Deuteronomy 6:5 adds "with all your might" (cf. 2 Kings 23:25) to emphasize that the devotion of the Israelite to Yahweh is to be that of the total person and existence.

It is clear here in the šᵉmaʿ and in the other texts which call for Israel's response of love that Israel loves Yahweh by keeping his commandments. Indeed, that is the purpose of the tôrāh in Deuteronomy—to show what it means to love God. "Love" in the Bible, whether on the part of man or of God, is not a feeling, but an action. And just as Yahweh "loved" Israel by delivering her out of Egypt and guiding her through the wilderness and giving her the promised land, so Israel is to love Yahweh by doing specific actions in obedience to Yahweh's will. In fact, all of life is to be a single-minded concentration on doing Yahweh's will, symbolized here in the šᵉmaʿ by the commands to write the law on the heart and to teach it diligently to the children and to discuss it in family and community life (6:6–7). The provision for phylacteries and mezuzahs, in 6:8f. originally might have been intended metaphorically, but later became a literal—and sometimes legalistic (cf. Matt. 23:5)—practice for the Jews. The šᵉmaʿ, along with Exodus 13:1–10, 11–16 and Deuteronomy 11:13–21 and sometimes the Decalogue, were written on parchment and enclosed in small boxes, worn on the arm and forehead during morning prayer, or attached to the doorpost of the house. The mention of them here in Deuteronomy 6:8f., however, simply emphasizes the importance of Yahweh's words as a guide for all of life. Israel is to love Yahweh in return for his love, but the law then is understood as instruction in how to love God.

It is obvious that the relationship with Yahweh is therefore not understood legalistically in Deuteronomy. Yahweh has already made Israel his people. He has already redeemed them and given them a new life and made them his own possession. Israel is already God's son; he does not have to earn that title. But now Yahweh does not let Israel stumble along uncertainly by himself. He does not abandon his people and give them no further guidance. Now he continues to guide them by means of the tôrāh of Deuteronomy. He continues to point out the way in which they should walk. He continues to be near them through the words of the law (4:7), so that they can act wisely and thus enter into the fullness of life which Yahweh desires for them. The law is not a burden for Israel in Deuteronomy, but rather synonymous with the very presence of God. Like the Holy Spirit, the Counselor, in the Fourth Gospel, who will continue to teach and sustain the disciples in that relationship which they have had with Jesus (John 14:15–26), the law is the continuation of Yahweh's relationship with his people and his ongoing personal guidance of them. The law is therefore laid upon Israel's heart, where the intimate personal relationship with Yahweh is played out, and obedience to the law is the manifestation of Israel's love for her Lord. It is not unlike the Fourth Gospel where love for Christ is shown by keeping his commandments (John 14:15, 21; cf. 1 John 5:2). Throughout Deuteronomy, love for God and obedience go together, because the law is the personal guidance of Yahweh, his teaching in how to love.

If Israel loves God in return for his love, if she obeys his words in Deuteronomy, then she will enter into that fullness of life, that good life in the good land with its rest, which Yahweh promised her. And how Yahweh longs for that! He pleads with his people to enter into the life he desires for them:

> Oh that they had such a mind (Hebrew: heart) as this always, to fear me and to keep all my commandments, that it might go well with them and with their children for ever (Deut. 5:29)!

Over and over again Yahweh tells his people that he desires loving obedience from them, because then they will live and take possession of the good land which Yahweh wants to give them (4:1; 5:33; 8:1; 16:20; 32:47). Then they will "prolong" their days in the land (4:40; 5:16; 6:2; 25:15). The constant phrase is: Obey the commandments "that it may go well with you" (4:40; 5:16, 29, 33; 6:3, 18; 12:25, 28). Yahweh wishes well for his people. He desires that they shall live (5:33; 22:7; 30:6, 16, 19). As in Ezekiel, he has no pleasure in the death of anyone (Ezek. 18:32). He begs his people to live, and the life he holds out to them is a life overflowing with blessing and goodness—that abundant life that awaits them at the end of their pilgrimage.

If Israel will be obedient, she will inherit the fullness of God's blessing (Deut. 28:1–14). If she will not obey, her end will be curse, destruction, death (27:15–26; 28:15–68). The blessing will be abundant life in the land, the fulfillment of God's purpose. The curse is the loss of the land (4:26; 11:17; 28:21) and finally destruction

off the face of the earth (6:15; 7:4; 8:19f.; 28:20, 24). Both blessing and curse are spelled out in the context of the land, and the way
to fullness of life in the land is loving obedience to God's commandments.

In Deuteronomy Israel is placed therefore before the necessity
of constant decision:

> See, I have set before you this day (which is every day in Deuter-
> onomy) life and good, death and evil. If you obey the commandments
> of the Lord your God . . . by loving the Lord your God, by walking
> in his ways, and by keeping his commandments . . . then you shall
> live and multiply, and the Lord your God will bless you in the land
> . . . But if your heart turns away . . . I declare to you this day, that
> you shall perish; you shall not live long in the land . . . I have set before
> you life and death, blessing and curse; therefore choose life, that you
> and your descendants may live . . . (Deut. 30:15–19; cf. Matt. 7:13–
> 14).

The choice is no "trifle" for Israel, but a matter of whether she
prospers or dies (32:47). The burning desire of Yahweh is that
Israel will choose rightly: "therefore choose life"; "that it may go
well with you"; it is for "your good" always (6:24; 10:13). The
yearning love of God for his people's good is almost overwhelming
in Deuteronomy. But it is not a love that will coerce Israel into her
choice. Rather, it is a love that asks the response of Israel's heart to
God's heart, Israel's love to God's love, Israel's loyalty to God's
loyalty. Israel is to love God, because God has first loved her.

## CHAPTER FIVE

# THE LAW OF LOVE AND THE COVENANT MEDIATOR

Israel is to love the Lord her God with all her heart and soul and might. She is to do so, not to earn her relationship with God, but because she already has been chosen as his people through his acts of love. She acts out her love in return for God's love by obeying his commandments. The law of Deuteronomy is the explication of what it means to love God.

It is not surprising therefore that Deuteronomy's law embraces the totality of Israel's existence. We find in the book not only what we would term "religious laws"—laws concerning worship (chap. 12; 16:21—17:1; 26:1–15; 27:1–8), idolatry (chap. 13; 17:2–7), clean and unclean food (14:3–21), tithes (14:22–29), the year of release (15:1–11), offerings (15:19–23), vows (23:21–23), festivals (16:1–17), priests (18:1–8), and prophets (18:15–22). We also find laws concerning the duties of judges (16:18–20; 17:8–13) and kings (17:14–20), laws about homicide (19:1–13; 21:1–9) and theft (19:14; 24:7) and false witness (19:15–21). There are laws regulating the conduct of war (chap. 20; 21:10–14; 23:9–14) and the life of the family (21:15–17, 18–21; 24:1–5; 25:5–10), laws concerning sexual activity (22:13–30; 25:11–12) and financial transactions (23:19f.; 24:6, 10–13; 25:13–16). No area of Israel's life is excluded from regulation by Yahweh, because Israel's commitment to her covenant Lord is to be a total commitment.

To love God with all one's heart and soul and might means first of all, in Deuteronomy, to regard God as the sovereign over the whole of life; there is no sphere of human existence which Deuteronomy would consider extraneous to regulation by Yahweh or in which human wisdom alone should be exercised. Israel's manner of life in Deuteronomy is a revealed way, unattainable through the human wisdom and knowledge of any other folk (4:6–8).

It is one of the hallmarks of Deuteronomy therefore that its *tôrāh* constantly warns Israel against following the customs of other peoples and worshiping other gods. In one sense, Deuteronomy is a long exegesis on the first commandment of the Decalogue, "You shall have no other gods before me" (5:7). As von Rad has stated, the work never loses sight of the enemy: its principal fight is against the Canaanite gods of fertility, whom Israel was constantly tempted to worship at the high places throughout the land. The repeated command is therefore that she must not "follow after (go after) other (foreign) gods" (6:14; 8:19; 11:28; 13:2; 28:14), or "serve/worship other gods" (7:4; 11:16; 13:2, 6, 13; 17:3 [astral deities of Assyria are referred to in 17:3b]; 28:14, 36, 64; 29:26; cf. 4:19; etc.). Of course, the law of centralization of worship has its basis in this concern.

Yahweh, says Deuteronomy, is a "jealous God" (4:24; 5:9; 6:15; cf. 29:20; 32:16, 21), a characterization apparently present in Israel's theology from the earliest (cf. Exod. 20:5; 34:14; Josh. 24:19) to the latest times. It is a covenantal expression, rooted in the facts that Yahweh has chosen Israel to be his own possession and that Israel has freely accepted that elected status. But primarily the term has to do with Yahweh's purpose in the world. The word for "jealousy" (*qînāh*) and "zeal" are identical in the Hebrew, and Yahweh's election of Israel is an expression of his zeal to accomplish his purpose. The purpose is, as we have seen, one of pure love, according to Deuteronomy—to give Israel a life of abundance in her place of rest. Thus the picture of the jealous God in Deuteronomy is almost that of some brooding Presence, encircling, bending over his people and sheltering them from all who would invade their life (cf. 32:10–12).

Deuteronomy therefore legislates against the imitation of any Canaanite or foreign custom (12:29–31). For example, the laws concerning clean and unclean animals (14:3–20) exclude from Israel's diet those animals which were considered sacred in foreign cults, just as the strange law in Deuteronomy 14:21b rejects a Ugaritic magical practice. The law of Deuteronomy 14:1–2 prohibits rituals practiced in foreign cults of the dead, and the strange prohibition of Deuteronomy 22:5 rejects masquerading practices known in the cult of Astarte. Similarly, the laws of Deuteronomy 22:9–11 prohibit foreign magical rites. Magic is strictly forbidden in Israel, along with soothsaying and divination (18:9–14), because it is foreign practice intended to coerce the deity, whereas Yahweh is sovereign Lord, who can be loved and obeyed but never manipulated.

Deuteronomy never wavers from its absolute prohibition of foreign worship. The consistent penalty for idolatry and for leading others into idolatry is death (chap. 13). This is carried to its ultimate extreme in the ancient stipulation of *herem*, which Deuteronomy revives from the traditions of the Holy War and which decreed that all prizes of war were to be "devoted" or sacrificed to Yahweh (7:1–5, 25f; 20:10–18; cf. Josh. 6:18—7:26; 1 Sam. 15). Certainly there was no way Israel could carry out such legislation in the seventh century B.C., and there is some doubt that in fact she ever practiced it. Thus what we have in the Deuteronomic law of *herem* is a theological statement: all foreign influence, practices, worship, mixed marriages are forbidden to Israel, and the reason for such exclusivism is clearly stated in Deuteronomy 7:4, 25 and 20:18.

The concern lying behind it all is the sole worship of Yahweh, and Deuteronomy revives the language of the Holy War to show the radical nature of that concern. No one would now countenance such language, even in theory, but the intention behind the law is to wipe out from Israel's life all those practices, revived during the time of Manasseh, which would lure her away from her sole loyalty to her God.

Deuteronomy is also a prolonged commentary on the meaning of the second commandment of the Decalogue (5:8–10; Exod. 20:4–6). In Deuteronomy 7:5 and 12:3 (cf. 16:21), Israel is commanded to break down all Canaanite altars, to dash in pieces their pillars, to hew down their Asherim, and burn their graven images with fire. Asherim were upright wooden cult objects used in the worship of Asherah, an important fertility deity of Phoenicia and Canaan. Pillars or *maṣṣēbôt* were stone cult objects of the fertility religions. Israel is thus commanded to do away with all cultic objects and altars of such nature religions. Such a command seems irrelevant to us, but the concept of God which lies behind it is of utmost importance. The belief of the fertility religions was that the deity could be manifested through the media of objects and phenomena in the created world, much as some today think they can find God through nature or art. The second commandment and Deuteronomy as a whole are the most radical attack on this concept. Nothing in all creation, it is said, is adequate to serve as a medium of revelation of Yahweh—nothing "in heaven above, or that is on the earth beneath, or that is in the water under the earth" (5:8).

Rather, Yahweh is to be found only at the place which he chooses, where he puts his name, and through the medium of his revealing word: "You heard the sound of words, but saw no form; there was only a voice" (4:12). Israel is to reject all natural religion for the worship of the invisible God alone, and she is to know her God only from the historical deeds and words in which he has chosen to reveal himself. In the *tôrāh* of Deuteronomy, Israel is called to give up all comfort and oneness with the world, for the sake of fellowship with God. The relationship of love to which she is called is an exclusive relationship in which the world is taken away from her, but then returned a hundred fold in the reward of abundant life in the land (cf. Matt. 19:16–30).

Yahweh is to be the sole sovereign over Israel's life, the recipient of all her love. This sovereignty lies behind the most varied of Deuteronomy's commands. For example, Israel cannot eat meat with the blood in it (12:16, 23f.; 15:23), because the blood is the bearer of the life, and Yahweh is the Lord over all living things (cf. 32:39). Again, Israel is commanded to set aside three cities of refuge for the manslayer who has unintentionally killed a fellow Israelite (4:41–43; 19:1–10). There the hunted man can flee and escape the blood-revenge from the deceased's relatives. Thus there is a sphere of justice, beyond the justice of men, which belongs to Yahweh alone. Or further, Israel must grant a year of release every seven years to Israelite debtors and slaves (15:1–3, 12ff.), not only because they belong to Yahweh as members of his people, but also because Yahweh places a final limit on the accumulation of human wealth and power. In every area of life, Yahweh holds final sway; he even legislates against secret sins, which men think they can do unnoticed, by placing an automatic curse upon them (27:15–26).

Deuteronomy also shares with the rest of the Bible the belief that God is loved by loving one's neighbor. Thus when it is asked how

Israel can respond to the love which Yahweh showed her in the exodus, the reply is that she can show the same mercy toward those who are helpless in her society—the slave (15:15), the sojourner or stranger (10:18f.), the orphan, and the widow (24:17–18, 19–22). The ancient world, like our world, understood justice in terms of power. But Yahweh has shown in his actions toward Israel that he is the God who cares for the weak, who "executes justice for the fatherless and the widow, and loves the sojourner, giving him food and clothing" (10:18). Therefore Israel is to act in the same manner: "for you were sojourners in the land of Egypt" (10:19); "you shall remember that you were a slave in the land of Egypt, and the Lord redeemed you" (15:15; cf. 24:18, 22).

This concern for the poor and helpless is a persistent note in Deuteronomy (14:28f.; 16:11, 14; 24:12f., 14f.; 26:12–15), and thus we have the phenomenon of a society shaped by the mercy of God. That mercy is not limited to Israelites alone: there is consistent concern shown for the rights and food and faith of the alien, who had no legal right in Israel (1:16; 5:14; 10:18f.; 14:21, 29; 16:11, 14; 23:7–8; 24:14, 17, 19, 21; 26:11, 13; 27:19; 29:10f; 31:12). Indeed, the mercy extended to Israel in the exodus is even to be shown to animals, and the command to give rest to one's ox and ass is, in Deuteronomy's version of the Decalogue, based on the remembrance of the deliverance from Egypt (5:12–15).

Israelite society was to be permeated by a spirit of kindness and helpfulness toward one's neighbor. Therefore a neighbor was to be aided in recovering a lost animal or other property (22:1–4). He was to be protected against injury which would cause strife between households (22:8). He was not to be subjected to usury (23:19), or deprived of the products of his labor (23:24f.). He was not to be held responsible for another's crime (24:16), or deprived of his means of livelihood (24:6). His inherited plot of land was to be his alone, and he was not to be cheated out of it (19:14). Even his dignity and truthfulness were to be honored and not demeaned (24:10f.).

Israel's society was to manifest the same righteousness and justice that Yahweh had manifested toward her. Thus the merchant was not to cheat his customers by the use of inaccurate weights and measures (25:13–16), and the fact that commercial dealings were understood as religious matters is emphasized by the reference to dishonesty as an "abomination" (a cultic term) to Yahweh (25:16; cf. Amos 8:5; Isa. 1:21–22; Hos. 12:7–8; Ezek. 45:10–12). The courts of law were to follow "justice, and only justice" (Deut. 16:20), and therefore no man could be convicted of a crime on the evidence of only one witness (19:15). False witnesses were condemned to suffer the punishment that they had thought to bring on the innocent (19:16–21). The guilty could not be given excessive or private punishment (25:1–3), the concern being that even a criminal should not be degraded by an unjust exercise of power. Judges especially had heavy responsibility that legal rights not be perverted: "you shall not show partiality; and you shall not take a bribe, for a bribe blinds the eyes of the wise and subverts the cause of the righteous" (16:19). Righteousness was essential to Israel's inheritance of God's good gifts in the land (16:20).

The noteworthy fact is, however, to what extent Deuteronomy goes beyond the bounds of legal justice and calls for the exercise of love within Israelite society. Relationships between human beings are characterized by devotion and love between master and slave (15:16), between husband and wife (21:15f.), between citizen and sojourner (10:19).

Nowhere is Deuteronomy's emphasis on love between human beings more evident than in its regulations concerning slaves and poor. No runaway foreign slave could be forced to return to his former master, and he was to be allowed to dwell in Israel in the place of his choosing (23:15f.) and not be enslaved again. Hebrew slaves were to be released in the seventh year: Yahweh had freed Israel from slavery in Egypt and therefore no Israelite was to be enslaved permanently, though he could sell himself for six years to pay off his debts (15:12–18). But the remarkable fact was the manner in which the Hebrew slave was to be released: he was to be given liberal gifts of meat and grain and wine (v. 13f.), and he was to be released gladly, with gratitude for his six years of service (v. 18). In short, relationships with slaves were matters of the heart, and it is recognized that there may even be such a bond of devotion between master and slave that the slave will not wish to be released, although that is a choice for the slave, and not the master to make (v. 16f.).

## CHAPTER SIX

## JEREMIAH THE PROPHET LIKE MOSE[S]

In the Old Testament there are two extended reflections on the wor[d] of God in Deuteronomy. Both show how Israel responded to tha[t] word and the result of her response. Both show how Yahweh kep[t] his word and promised Israel a future. The first of these is the De[u]teronomic history. The second is the Book of Jeremiah.

To many that will seem like a very rash statement, because n[o] problem in Old Testament study has been more vexing than th[e] relationship of Jeremiah to Deuteronomy and the Deuteronom[ic] reform. Because of the uncertainties attending that relationship, w[e] have no scholarly concensus about the dating of Jeremiah's minist[ry] or about the nature of the genuine material in his book. Yet if w[e] examine the content of Jeremiah's oracles in themselves—witho[ut] first worrying about the problem of dates—the evidence is almo[st] overwhelming that the prophet is concerned precisely with Deute[r]onomy's concerns: with the word spoken to Israel's heart and th[e] response of her heart to the one Lord. Indeed, it is that word writt[en] upon his own heart with which Jeremiah struggles all his life, as h[e] tries to come to terms with his prophetic calling. And it is final[ly] when Jeremiah resolves the problems of his own heart and of th[e] heart of his nation that he sees the future which Yahweh has in sto[re] for his chosen people. We turn now to the attempt to make the[se] matters clear.

The first key to the Book of Jeremiah is the account of the prop[h]et's initial call in 1:4–10. The account forms the legitimizatio[n] of Jeremiah's ministry, and it sets forth the nature both of Jeremiah[s] role and of Yahweh's activity in his time. It is stated in very simpl[e,] almost curt, terms, with no extraneous details. The words of Yahw[eh] are set in poetry, the rest of the account in prose.

The dialogue is an intimate exchange between the prophet a[nd] God. The prophet speaks neither of Isaiah's awesome Holy One

Deuteronomy is quite conscious of the sinful rationalizations possible in the human heart.

In regard to the poor, Deuteronomy looks forward to that fulfillment when there shall be no poor (15:4f.), but it recognizes quite realistically that in the meantime there will always be the needy and poverty-stricken who must be helped (v. 11). Especially was the problem of poverty acute from the time of the prophets on, when a great gap between the rich and poor developed and state taxes became increasingly burdensome. Poor people were therefore often forced to borrow heavily to pay off their debts.

Deuteronomy therefore extends the "year of release," which originally applied only to the land, also to the cancellation of debts (15:2, 9). But those who lend are to pay no attention to the nearness of the year of release. They are to lend to the poor man whatever he may need (vv. 8–9), freely and ungrudgingly (v. 10), with a wide open hand (v. 11). Such generosity is a matter of an open heart (v. 10), of a love manifested toward one's fellow, which flows forth in sharing.

"We love because he first loved us" (1 John 4:19): no book of the Old Testament better expresses that spirit than does the Book of Deuteronomy. Israel's response to the love of God must be heartfelt love within her society, manifested to every class and condition of person. Indeed, her humaneness is to spill over into her treatment of the world of nature (20:19f.; 22:6–7; 25:4); she acts out her love for God by responsibility for his world. In sole obedience to Yahweh's teaching, Israel acknowledges his sovereignty, and gives back to him her total commitment of heart and soul and strength. It surely is the same love to which our Lord calls his church.

We finally must say some words about the figure of Moses in Deuteronomy, whom the Gospel according to Matthew, for example, makes a foreshadowing of Jesus of Nazareth (see author's book, *The Old Testament and the Proclamation of the Gospel*).

Moses is the first and greatest of the prophets, according to Deuteronomy 34:10–12 (cf. Num. 12:6–8). As such, he is the mediator between God and Israel, receiving the *tôrāh* from Yahweh, when Israel is unable to stand before God's glory because of her sin (Deut. 5:22–27). Like the prophets who come after him (cf.

Amos 7:1–6; Jer. 7:16; Ezek. 13:4f.), Moses is also the intercessor for Israel before Yahweh. It is his ascetic pleading before the Lord which turns aside Yahweh's wrath toward his rebellious people in the wilderness (Deut. 9:25ff.) and at Mt. Horeb (9:13ff.; 10:10f.). But significantly, Moses is a suffering mediator for his people. Contrary to the tradition in Numbers 20:11f., in which it is Moses' own sin which prevents his entrance into the promised land, Deuteronomy states that Moses remains outside of the land because of his people's sin (1:37; 3:26; 4:21). He bears their sin for them and dies outside of the land, in order that they may enter in and have life.

Deuteronomy further makes Moses the model of all true prophets, and it is promised in Deuteronomy 18:15ff. that after him, Yahweh will raise up a prophet like him, from among the Israelites, to whom Israel is to give heed. Probably every one of the classical prophets in Israel was understood to fulfill this role of the Mosaic successor; certainly Jeremiah was. Von Rad believes that even the Suffering Servant of Deutero-Isaiah is to be understood in the context of this tradition about the suffering Mosaic prophet-mediator (*Old Testament Theology, II.*)

By the time of the New Testament, we see evidence that the expectation of a "prophet like Moses" has taken on eschatological tones. There is the anticipation of a special prophet to come (cf. John 1:21, 25; 6:14; 7:40; 1 QS 9:10f.; 4 Q Testim. 5–8), and in Acts, Jesus is specifically identified with this eschatological prophet like Moses (Acts 3:22–26; cf. 7:37, 52) as well as with the figure of the Servant (3:26; 4:24–30).

Moses, in Deuteronomy, serves as a foreshadowing of the figure of Jesus. It is a significant analogy, for our Lord comes to us, proclaiming the *tôrāh* of the new covenant, on the new mount of revelation (Matt. 5—7). Like Moses, he calls for the total commitment of our heart and soul and mind and strength in love to God and neighbor, in order that we may enter into our final inheritance of abundant life. But that is not a legalistic call, any more than Moses' was. It is a call which assures us that already, this day, we are the people of God, redeemed out of slavery and given the possibility of new life. It is a call which assures us, as Moses did Israel, that God is with us and that we therefore need never fear any threat or enemy. It is

a call which carries with it God's heartfelt yearning for our always and the power to answer in obedience. It is a call which us before the decision of whether we shall have life or death. Moses, our covenant mediator also intercedes for us before Father, and lays down his life for our sin. But unlike Moses, dies and whose grave remains unknown in order to prevent worship of him (Deut. 34:5f.), our covenant mediator is raised exalted to the right hand of the Father, as the Lord whom we ship and adore. Jesus Christ has won the victory which Moses only dimly foresee (cf. Deut. 3:23–27). In him, the journey of finds its final goal and fulfillment.

Israel nor of Ezekiel's bizarre and stunning *kābôd Yahweh*. Consequently there is nothing of Isaiah's crushing sense of personal guilt or of Ezekiel's speechless stupor. Jeremiah talks person to person with the covenant Lord and Father of his people.

The scene reminds one of Moses' intimate dialogues with God, and it is quite clear from the details of the account that Jeremiah understands himself called to be the prophet like Moses of Deuteronomy 18:15–22. Many commentators have noted this analogy (see especially Holladay, *JBL*, 1964): verse 9, "I have put my words in your mouth," and verse 7, "whatever I command you you shall speak" are paralleled in Deuteronomy 18:18; this combination of "command" and "speak" (cf. Jer. 14:14) is found in Exodus 7:2 in connection with Moses. Jeremiah's objection to his call in verse 6, is very similar to that of Moses (Exod. 4:10), both accounts containing a precative interjection followed by an emphatic personal pronoun. Only Jeremiah 1:9; 5:14; and Deuteronomy 18:18 use the verb *nātan* (to give; RSV "put") instead of *sûm* (to put) in such a context.

If we reflect on Jeremiah and the figure of Moses as he is presented to us in Deuteronomy, it is immediately clear that there are other similarities between the two. Both intercede for Israel before the Lord (cf. Jer. 7:16; 11:14; 14:11; 15:11; 18:20), both are suffering mediators before God, and the suffering of both finally influences the portrayal of the Suffering Servant in Second Isaiah. Both are covenant mediators, and it is not too much to say that Jeremiah proclaimed the new covenant to come (31:31–34) precisely because he was the prophet like Moses. There are also a number of parallels between Jeremiah's poetry and the Song of Moses in Deuteronomy 32 (see Driver and Holladay).

But returning to Jeremiah's call itself, which is almost universally recognized to be genuine with the prophet, any student of Deuteronomy is struck immediately by Deuteronomic language in this passage. First, there is the familiar "this day" in verse 10. More important is verse 8: "Be not afraid of them, for I am with you to deliver you" (cf. 1:19; 15:20). That is the language of the Holy War, with which we became so familiar in Deuteronomy (cf. Deut. 1:21, 29; 3:2, 22; 7:18, 21; 20:1; 31:6, 8). The God who calls Jeremiah is the Divine Warrior, the incomparable Mighty Man (*gibbōr*), whom we met in Deuteronomy (cf. the use of *gibbōr* in Deut. 10:17 and its derivative at 3:24). In one passage, the prophet specifically says so:

> But the Lord is with me as a dread warrior;
> therefore my persecutors will stumble (Jer. 20:11; cf. 14:9).

It is no accident therefore that Jeremiah 20:12 continues by calling God "the Lord of hosts," again a Holy War appellative, and that it is to such a Divine Warrior that Jeremiah commits his cause. "Yahweh of hosts" is used as a title for God throughout the Book of Jeremiah, and the prophet understands that title in the context of the sacral battle (so interpret 6:9; 9:7; 16:9; 23:15, etc.).

We are now beginning to discern the outlines of Jeremiah's understanding of his call. He is the prophet like Moses, promised in Deuteronomy 18:15–22, and he will be defended in his role by the Divine Warrior of the Holy War, exactly as Moses and Israel were to be defended according to Deuteronomy. Moreover, Jeremiah hears in his call that he has been set apart (RSV "consecrated") for such a role even before he was formed (cf. Ps. 139:13; Job 10:11) in the womb (cf. Isa. 49:1, 5). The purpose and meaning of his life lie in his becoming this Mosaic prophet.

There is more here. We have noted the intimacy of the account, paralleling Moses' intimacy with Yahweh, and the fact that Yahweh "gives" his word into Jeremiah's mouth (Jer. 1:9; cf. Exod. 4:12, 15). From other passages in the book, we know that Jeremiah conceives of this encounter as having taken place in the heavenly council of the Lord (23:18; cf. 18:20). Indeed in much of prophetic thought there is a royal court scene taking place in heaven (cf. 1 Kings 22:19ff.; Isa. 6; 40:1–8; Job 1:6–12). Very often it is a judgment court of law. And it has been widely recognized by scholars that the prophets are understood in the Old Testament as the messengers of this heavenly council or court, responsible for declaring on earth the verdict of the divine court (cf. Hos. 4:1ff.; Isa. 41:1ff.; Mic. 6:1ff.; Jer. 2:4ff.). Such is Jeremiah. He has stood in the council of Yahweh to hear and perceive his word. It is there that Yahweh has put his word in his mouth. But as is clear in Jeremiah 23:18–20, that word is of a Holy War, in which the storm of the Lord breaks forth in wrath against the people of Judah. The

Deuteronomy is quite conscious of the sinful rationalizations possible in the human heart.

In regard to the poor, Deuteronomy looks forward to that fulfillment when there shall be no poor (15:4f.), but it recognizes quite realistically that in the meantime there will always be the needy and poverty-stricken who must be helped (v. 11). Especially was the problem of poverty acute from the time of the prophets on, when a great gap between the rich and poor developed and state taxes became increasingly burdensome. Poor people were therefore often forced to borrow heavily to pay off their debts.

Deuteronomy therefore extends the "year of release," which originally applied only to the land, also to the cancellation of debts (15:2, 9). But those who lend are to pay no attention to the nearness of the year of release. They are to lend to the poor man whatever he may need (vv. 8–9), freely and ungrudgingly (v. 10), with a wide open hand (v. 11). Such generosity is a matter of an open heart (v. 10), of a love manifested toward one's fellow, which flows forth in sharing.

"We love because he first loved us" (1 John 4:19): no book of the Old Testament better expresses that spirit than does the Book of Deuteronomy. Israel's response to the love of God must be heartfelt love within her society, manifested to every class and condition of person. Indeed, her humaneness is to spill over into her treatment of the world of nature (20:19f.; 22:6–7; 25:4); she acts out her love for God by responsibility for his world. In sole obedience to Yahweh's teaching, Israel acknowledges his sovereignty, and gives back to him her total commitment of heart and soul and strength. It surely is the same love to which our Lord calls his church.

We finally must say some words about the figure of Moses in Deuteronomy, whom the Gospel according to Matthew, for example, makes a foreshadowing of Jesus of Nazareth (see author's book, *The Old Testament and the Proclamation of the Gospel*).

Moses is the first and greatest of the prophets, according to Deuteronomy 34:10–12 (cf. Num. 12:6–8). As such, he is the mediator between God and Israel, receiving the *tôrāh* from Yahweh, when Israel is unable to stand before God's glory because of her sin (Deut. 5:22–27). Like the prophets who come after him (cf.

Amos 7:1–6; Jer. 7:16; Ezek. 13:4f.), Moses is also the intercessor for Israel before Yahweh. It is his ascetic pleading before the Lord which turns aside Yahweh's wrath toward his rebellious people in the wilderness (Deut. 9:25ff.) and at Mt. Horeb (9:13ff.; 10:10f.). But significantly, Moses is a suffering mediator for his people. Contrary to the tradition in Numbers 20:11f., in which it is Moses' own sin which prevents his entrance into the promised land, Deuteronomy states that Moses remains outside of the land because of his people's sin (1:37; 3:26; 4:21). He bears their sin for them and dies outside of the land, in order that they may enter in and have life.

Deuteronomy further makes Moses the model of all true prophets, and it is promised in Deuteronomy 18:15ff. that after him, Yahweh will raise up a prophet like him, from among the Israelites, to whom Israel is to give heed. Probably every one of the classical prophets in Israel was understood to fulfill this role of the Mosaic successor; certainly Jeremiah was. Von Rad believes that even the Suffering Servant of Deutero-Isaiah is to be understood in the context of this tradition about the suffering Mosaic prophet-mediator (*Old Testament Theology, II.*)

By the time of the New Testament, we see evidence that the expectation of a "prophet like Moses" has taken on eschatological tones. There is the anticipation of a special prophet to come (cf. John 1:21, 25; 6:14; 7:40; 1 QS 9:10f.; 4 Q Testim. 5–8), and in Acts, Jesus is specifically identified with this eschatological prophet like Moses (Acts 3:22–26; cf. 7:37, 52) as well as with the figure of the Servant (3:26; 4:24–30).

Moses, in Deuteronomy, serves as a foreshadowing of the figure of Jesus. It is a significant analogy, for our Lord comes to us, proclaiming the *tôrāh* of the new covenant, on the new mount of revelation (Matt. 5—7). Like Moses, he calls for the total commitment of our heart and soul and mind and strength in love to God and neighbor, in order that we may enter into our final inheritance of abundant life. But that is not a legalistic call, any more than Moses' was. It is a call which assures us that already, this day, we are the people of God, redeemed out of slavery and given the possibility of new life. It is a call which assures us, as Moses did Israel, that God is with us and that we therefore need never fear any threat or enemy. It is a call which carries with it God's heartfelt yearning for our good always and the power to answer in obedience. It is a call which sets us before the decision of whether we shall have life or death. Like Moses, our covenant mediator also intercedes for us before the Father, and lays down his life for our sin. But unlike Moses, who dies and whose grave remains unknown in order to prevent any worship of him (Deut. 34:5f.), our covenant mediator is raised and exalted to the right hand of the Father, as the Lord whom we worship and adore. Jesus Christ has won the victory which Moses could only dimly foresee (cf. Deut. 3:23–27). In him, the journey of Israel finds its final goal and fulfillment.

# JEREMIAH THE PROPHET LIKE MOSES

In the Old Testament there are two extended reflections on the word of God in Deuteronomy. Both show how Israel responded to that word and the result of her response. Both show how Yahweh kept his word and promised Israel a future. The first of these is the Deuteronomic history. The second is the Book of Jeremiah.

To many that will seem like a very rash statement, because no problem in Old Testament study has been more vexing than the relationship of Jeremiah to Deuteronomy and the Deuteronomic reform. Because of the uncertainties attending that relationship, we have no scholarly concensus about the dating of Jeremiah's ministry or about the nature of the genuine material in his book. Yet if we examine the content of Jeremiah's oracles in themselves—without first worrying about the problem of dates—the evidence is almost overwhelming that the prophet is concerned precisely with Deuteronomy's concerns: with the word spoken to Israel's heart and the response of her heart to the one Lord. Indeed, it is that word written upon his own heart with which Jeremiah struggles all his life, as he tries to come to terms with his prophetic calling. And it is finally when Jeremiah resolves the problems of his own heart and of the heart of his nation that he sees the future which Yahweh has in store for his chosen people. We turn now to the attempt to make these matters clear.

The first key to the Book of Jeremiah is the account of the prophet's initial call in 1:4–10. The account forms the legitimization of Jeremiah's ministry, and it sets forth the nature both of Jeremiah's role and of Yahweh's activity in his time. It is stated in very simple, almost curt, terms, with no extraneous details. The words of Yahweh are set in poetry, the rest of the account in prose.

The dialogue is an intimate exchange between the prophet and God. The prophet speaks neither of Isaiah's awesome Holy One of

Israel nor of Ezekiel's bizarre and stunning *kābôd Yahweh*. Consequently there is nothing of Isaiah's crushing sense of personal guilt or of Ezekiel's speechless stupor. Jeremiah talks person to person with the covenant Lord and Father of his people.

The scene reminds one of Moses' intimate dialogues with God, and it is quite clear from the details of the account that Jeremiah understands himself called to be the prophet like Moses of Deuteronomy 18:15–22. Many commentators have noted this analogy (see especially Holladay, *JBL*, 1964): verse 9, "I have put my words in your mouth," and verse 7, "whatever I command you you shall speak" are paralleled in Deuteronomy 18:18; this combination of "command" and "speak" (cf. Jer. 14:14) is found in Exodus 7:2 in connection with Moses. Jeremiah's objection to his call in verse 6, is very similar to that of Moses (Exod. 4:10), both accounts containing a precative interjection followed by an emphatic personal pronoun. Only Jeremiah 1:9; 5:14; and Deuteronomy 18:18 use the verb *nātan* (to give; RSV "put") instead of *sûm* (to put) in such a context.

If we reflect on Jeremiah and the figure of Moses as he is presented to us in Deuteronomy, it is immediately clear that there are other similarities between the two. Both intercede for Israel before the Lord (cf. Jer. 7:16; 11:14; 14:11; 15:11; 18:20), both are suffering mediators before God, and the suffering of both finally influences the portrayal of the Suffering Servant in Second Isaiah. Both are covenant mediators, and it is not too much to say that Jeremiah proclaimed the new covenant to come (31:31–34) precisely because he was the prophet like Moses. There are also a number of parallels between Jeremiah's poetry and the Song of Moses in Deuteronomy 32 (see Driver and Holladay).

But returning to Jeremiah's call itself, which is almost universally recognized to be genuine with the prophet, any student of Deuteronomy is struck immediately by Deuteronomic language in this passage. First, there is the familiar "this day" in verse 10. More important is verse 8: "Be not afraid of them, for I am with you to deliver you" (cf. 1:19; 15:20). That is the language of the Holy War, with which we became so familiar in Deuteronomy (cf. Deut. 1:21, 29; 3:2, 22; 7:18, 21; 20:1; 31:6, 8). The God who calls Jeremiah is the Divine Warrior, the incomparable Mighty Man (*gibbōr*), whom we met in Deuteronomy (cf. the use of *gibbōr* in Deut. 10:17 and its derivative at 3:24). In one passage, the prophet specifically says so:

> But the Lord is with me as a dread warrior;
> therefore my persecutors will stumble (Jer. 20:11; cf. 14:9).

It is no accident therefore that Jeremiah 20:12 continues by calling God "the Lord of hosts," again a Holy War appellative, and that it is to such a Divine Warrior that Jeremiah commits his cause. "Yahweh of hosts" is used as a title for God throughout the Book of Jeremiah, and the prophet understands that title in the context of the sacral battle (so interpret 6:9; 9:7; 16:9; 23:15, etc.).

We are now beginning to discern the outlines of Jeremiah's understanding of his call. He is the prophet like Moses, promised in Deuteronomy 18:15–22, and he will be defended in his role by the Divine Warrior of the Holy War, exactly as Moses and Israel were to be defended according to Deuteronomy. Moreover, Jeremiah hears in his call that he has been set apart (RSV "consecrated") for such a role even before he was formed (cf. Ps. 139:13; Job 10:11) in the womb (cf. Isa. 49:1, 5). The purpose and meaning of his life lie in his becoming this Mosaic prophet.

There is more here. We have noted the intimacy of the account, paralleling Moses' intimacy with Yahweh, and the fact that Yahweh "gives" his word into Jeremiah's mouth (Jer. 1:9; cf. Exod. 4:12, 15). From other passages in the book, we know that Jeremiah conceives of this encounter as having taken place in the heavenly council of the Lord (23:18; cf. 18:20). Indeed in much of prophetic thought there is a royal court scene taking place in heaven (cf. 1 Kings 22:19ff.; Isa. 6; 40:1–8; Job 1:6–12). Very often it is a judgment court of law. And it has been widely recognized by scholars that the prophets are understood in the Old Testament as the messengers of this heavenly council or court, responsible for declaring on earth the verdict of the divine court (cf. Hos. 4:1ff.; Isa. 41:1ff.; Mic. 6:1ff.; Jer. 2:4ff.). Such is Jeremiah. He has stood in the council of Yahweh to hear and perceive his word. It is there that Yahweh has put his word in his mouth. But as is clear in Jeremiah 23:18–20, that word is of a Holy War, in which the storm of the Lord breaks forth in wrath against the people of Judah. The false prophets proclaim "peace" to the people (23:17, RSV "well"; 4:10; 6:14). Jeremiah, who has truly received the word of the Lord, knows it is war.

It has often been recognized that the Book of Jeremiah contains much language from the Holy War (see Miller): the phrase "sanctify war" (6:4 [RSV "prepare war"]; 51:27; cf. 22:7); stereotyped commands to get ready for battle (46:3f.; 49:8, 14, 30f.; 50:14f., 21, 29; 51:11, 27); commands to the innocent to flee (4:6f; 6:1; 49:8, 30; 50:8; 51:6). Soggin maintains that the announcement that Yahweh declares Holy War *against Israel* is probably new with Jeremiah (cf. Mic. 3:5), and it is probable that Jeremiah used such language because of the influence of Deuteronomy. All the preexilic prophets announced God's judgment on Israel, but Jeremiah for the first time uses the technical terminology of the Holy War (6:4).

When Jeremiah receives this word of the Lord in the heavenly council concerning the Holy War, it is a word which he receives on his "heart." Deuteronomy repeatedly emphasizes that its *tôrāh* is to be upon Israel's heart (Deut. 4:39; 6:6; 11:18; 30:14; 32:46). Thus Jeremiah can say that he "ate" Yahweh's words, and they became "the delight" of his "heart" (Jer. 15:16), that the word "is in" his "heart as it were a burning fire" (20:9), that his "heart is broken" within him "because of the Lord and because of his holy words" (23:9).

The word which Yahweh lays on Jeremiah's heart is a word of Holy War against the people. Therefore, in a later period, Jeremiah cries out:

> My anguish, my anguish! I writhe in pain!
>   Oh, the walls of my heart!
> My heart is beating wildly;
>   I cannot keep silent;
> for I hear the sound of the trumpet,
>   the alarm of war (Jer. 4:19).

The war of the word is literally internalized within the prophet himself. Therefore his "heart is sick within" him (8:18), and "for the wound of the daughter of (his) people, his heart is wounded" (8:21). The word on his heart is one of "violence and destruction," and therefore the people fight back at him (20:8, 10), but Yahweh is with him as that "dread warrior," the "Lord of hosts" who delivers him from his enemies.

As in Deuteronomy 8:2 (cf. 13:3), Yahweh tests the heart (Jer. 11: 20=20:12; 17:10), and it is precisely because the false prophets do not have Yahweh's word on their heart that they are bogus preachers. Instead, they have "lies" in their hearts; they "prophesy the deceit of their own heart" (23:26); they speak visions of their own hearts (RSV "minds"; 23:16; 14:14). Yahweh has neither sent them nor spoken to them (23:21, 32), that is, he has not put his word on their hearts. Like the false prophet of Deuteronomy 13:1ff., they tell dreams which make the people go after other gods (Jer. 23:27f.).

Such, then, is Jeremiah's understanding of his initial call. He is the prophet like Moses, privy to the heavenly court, who has the word of Yahweh's Holy War against his people laid upon his heart, who must speak that word to whomever Yahweh sends him, and who is told that Yahweh, the Mighty Man of war, will fight for him and protect him against his enemies. The similarity with the motifs of Deuteronomy are too many to be accidental.

Before we draw any further conclusions from this evidence, we must note the other elements in Jeremiah's understanding of his initial call. First, he is appointed a prophet to the nations (1:5, 10a). Predestination, election, and consecration in the Bible are always for a task; there is no sense in which the one called is simply invited into fellowship with God. The communion is for the purpose of carrying out God's mission. Jeremiah is to speak to the nations, as well as to Israel.

Some have maintained that the text is faulty here and that "nations" is to be changed to "my nation," or that the phrase "to the nations" is to be omitted. But Jeremiah is certainly a prophet to the nations. He names Nebuchadnezzar of Babylonia the "servant" of Yahweh (27:6), and he proclaims the word of the Lord to the ambassadors of many lands (27:3ff.). Although some parts of the oracles to foreign nations in chapters 46—51 are from a later hand, there is much that is genuine in them: 46:3–12, 14–24; 47:2–7; 49:1–5, 23–27, 28–33, 35–38. Living in the age in which he did, there was no way in which Jeremiah could have proclaimed God's word without dealing with his entire Near Eastern world.

Further, in a decisive manner Jeremiah's message breaks the restrictions of Israelite nationalism. Perhaps only Second Isaiah emphasizes more the election history of Israel (cf. Jer. 2:4–13). Yet finally land, king, ark, temple are expendable for Jeremiah in the covenant relationship with God. God can be found as readily in Babylonia as in Judea, if he is sought with all the heart (29:13; cf. Deut. 4:29; Jer. 24:7). Mizpah can serve as well as Jerusalem for a political center; Gedaliah can be as acceptable as a Davidic king (40:6ff.). As in Deuteronomy, the ark is desacralized and is no longer necessary either to the Holy War or to Israel's worship (Jer. 3:16). The covenant with Yahweh bursts the bounds of place and institution, and though the land is never lost sight of, it now truly is framed by a universal vision. We must ask if that is not finally the outcome of a theology which is dealing with God's heart (23:20; 30:24; RSV "mind") and ours (cf. 32:39–41), the outcome of a true understanding of the faith of Deuteronomy. Certainly it is the direction in which the New Testament pushed Deuteronomy's proclamation.

Finally, in relation to Jeremiah's initial call, he is set "this day over nations and over kingdoms, to pluck up and to break down . . . to build and to plant" (1:10; most scholars omit "to destroy and to overthrow" as extraneous to the chiasmus). Jeremiah borrows the language of Isaiah 5:1–7 (cf. Ps. 80:8ff.) to affirm that Yahweh has "planted" the vine of Israel (Jer. 2:21; cf. 11:17; 12:2 to which cf. Isa. 29:13). But his prophetic call lays upon him the task of announcing that Yahweh is plucking up and breaking down the vine (cf. Deut. 29:28) in the divine war against Israel (cf. Jer. 31:28; 45:4). As we shall see, it will not be until the uprooting is accomplished that the building and planting will take place.

We must be cautious in interpreting this call to Jeremiah for our preaching and teaching. Neil characterizes the call as "the gentle but persistent prodding of what we should call the still small voice of conscience."[1] Holladay writes, "Jeremiah would have been keenly struck by the promise given to Moses that a new prophet, like Moses, would be called by God from among the Israelites (Deut. 18:18), and the notion would have crossed his mind that the one whom God had intended might well be he."[2] There is no evidence that either approach captures the nature of the prophetic call. The prophets were not summoned by inner voices. Rather, as with all the prophets, the word comes to Jeremiah from outside himself (cf. Ezek. 2:9—3:3), apparently with no warning or preparation (cf. Amos 7:14f.). He does not welcome that word (cf. Isa. 6:11), and it is a burden to him all his life long (cf. Jer. 23:33ff.). But it is laid upon his heart as a burning fire, and try as he will to hold it in, he must speak it forth (Jer. 20:9).

Obviously many of the motifs in this call of Jeremiah bear the closest resemblance to theological motifs which we found in Deuteronomy. We therefore must ask if Jeremiah is dependent on Deuteronomy and what that does to the dating of his ministry.

In Jeremiah 1:1–3, we read that the word of the Lord came to Jeremiah in the thirteenth year of the reign of Josiah, which would be 627/26 B.C. Thus the call of the prophet would precede by five years the finding of the scroll of Deuteronomy (2 Kings 22—23). This dating has been called into question on several grounds however. 1) Some argue that the Foe from the North, predicted in Jeremiah 1:13ff. and in much of Jeremiah 4:5—6:30 is the Babylonians of 609 B.C. and following, and not the Scythians of 626, as was earlier thought. There is no certain evidence that Scythian tribes ever invaded Palestine. But since Jeremiah 1:13–15 is part of the call narrative, then the call must have been later than 626 B.C. 2) There are no oracles which can be assigned with confidence to the period of Josiah, 627–609 B.C., and there is no mention of Josiah's death, which would be surprising if Jeremiah were already engaged in his ministry. 3) There is no certain word in the book about the Deuteronomic reform, again surprising if Jeremiah were already preaching; Jeremiah 11:1–13 refers merely to the Sinai covenant.

Two suggestions have therefore been made on the basis of these arguments. 1) The reference to the "thirteenth year" of Josiah in Jeremiah 1:2 is a mistake for the original reading of the "twenty-third year." In this view Jeremiah began to prophesy about 617/16 B.C., when Nabopolassar of Babylonia was becoming strong, and the Foe from the North is the Babylonians (so Gordon, Bardtke, Gottwald). It should be noticed, however, that Jeremiah 25:3 also reads "thirteenth year," and it is doubtful that the same textual error would be made twice. 2) The reference to the thirteenth year in Jeremiah 1:2 is the date of the prophet's birth, and he began his ministry in

609 B.C. with his famous temple sermon, which is the first dated oracle in the book (7:1–15; cf. 26:1). Thus Jeremiah was seventeen or eighteen-years old at the time of his call, which fits his statement in 1:6 that he is a "youth" (so Hyatt, Holladay). This view carries much more weight than 1), and it would seem to be supported by the similarities between the call of Jeremiah and the motifs of Deuteronomy, since the scroll of Deuteronomy would first had to have been found. Holladay further argues that Jeremiah 15:16a is a reference to the finding of the scroll in the temple (*JBL*, March, 1966), and that one reason why Jeremiah wrote his own words down on a scroll (chap. 36) was because he was imitating the scroll of Deuteronomy. In addition, it must be noted that in 1:4–10, the motif of Yahweh's war against Judah would seem to imply that Jeremiah announced Yahweh's judgment against his people from the beginning. Such a message would not seem to fit the period of Josiah's reform. It would be much more appropriate from 609 B.C. on, when the reform had lapsed and the Babylonian threat had become clear.

Despite the force of such arguments, I think we have to take the text in its plainest meaning and conclude that Jeremiah received his initial call in 627/26 B.C. Certainly 1:13–15 is a later call, as indicated by "a second time" in verse 13; it belongs to that period when Jeremiah proclaimed the oracles concerning the Foe from the North, since it is the initial announcement concerning the coming of that Foe. There is nothing which argues against Jeremiah having proclaimed words of judgment in the period from 627–622 B.C., and the prophet received the word of Yahweh's war against Judah from the very first, as we have seen. But how can we account for the similarities between 1:4–10 and the theology of Deuteronomy, if the latter was found five years after Jeremiah's initial call? Indeed, how can we account for the copious Deuteronomic language throughout the Book of Jeremiah, which seems to indicate the presence of an extended Deuteronomic source in the book? (We shall discuss such a source more fully in the next chapter).

The solution to these problems, it seems, lies in Jeremiah's background. We are told in 1:1 that Jeremiah was the "son of Hilkiah, of the priests who were in Anathoth in the land of Benjamin." Hilkiah is not identical with the high priest by the same name, who found the scroll of Deuteronomy in the temple (2 Kings 22:8). However, we do know from Joshua 21:17–19 that Anathoth, located 3½ miles NNE of Jerusalem (modern Ras el-Kharrubeh), was one of the four Levitical cities set aside for priests in the tribe of Benjamin. We know further from 1 Kings 2:26f. that Abiathar, the descendant of Eli who was priest at the time of David, was banished to Anathoth for his opposition to Solomon. Therefore, Jeremiah may be a descendant of Abiathar, and though not a priest himself, his roots go back to Eli and the ancient amphictyonic center at Shiloh (cf. Jer. 7:12, 14). In short, Jeremiah is heir to the sacral, covenant traditions of the Israelite amphictyony.

Further, we must note that while Benjamin became a part of Judah after the division of the kingdom in 922 B.C., it nevertheless was a northern Rachel tribe (cf. Jer. 31:15). As such, Benjamin was heir to the amphictyonic and prophetic traditions of the North, with their scant regard for the Davidic kingship and temple (cf. 17:19–27; note v. 26). When the northern kingdom fell in 722/21 B.C., Benjamin remained intact as a part of Judah. Nevertheless, its loyalties were to the North, and it has often been pointed out with what sympathy Jeremiah, as a citizen of Benjamin, proclaimed the restoration of the northern kingdom (31:2–6, 7–9, 15–20, 21f.; 32:8, 44; 33:13; 50:17–28; cf. 6:1).

It may be, therefore, that the northern, amphictyonic, levitical traditions of Deuteronomy were preserved in the territory of Benjamin after 721 B.C. and that Jeremiah was heir to them in his hometown of Anathoth and in his priestly household, even before the scroll of Deuteronomy was found in the temple in 622/21 B.C. Those who date the beginning of the prophet's activity sometime after 622/21 B.C. have always assumed that Jeremiah was dependent on the *literary* entity of Deuteronomy for his understanding of himself as the prophet like Moses. But the traditions of Deuteronomy were kept alive among the heirs of the reform movement that formulated them in the first place, and those traditions were preserved in the territory of Benjamin. They were, indeed, as von Rad has maintained, the product of the country Levites. But there were also prophetic members and supporters of the reform movement of Deuteronomy, and Jeremiah was called in 627/26 B.C. to be one of them. In fact he was called to be the prophet like Moses of Deuteronomy 18:15–22.

## CHAPTER SEVEN

# THE SOURCES AND FORMATION
# OF THE BOOK

As the Book of Jeremiah now stands, it divides itself into four sections: 1) chapters 1—25: Jeremiah's prophecies against his own people; 2) chapters 26—45: a biography about Jeremiah, written in the third person; 3) chapters 46—51: prophecies against the foreign nations; 4) chapter 52: a historical appendix, parallel to 2 Kings 24:18—25:30.

In the LXX version of the book, chapters 46—51 are placed after 25:13, and the oracles of those chapters are in a different order. The LXX text is ⅛ shorter, and it is evident that the LXX is based upon a different manuscript tradition than that used by the Masoretes.

Modern critical study of the Book of Jeremiah began with Duhm's 1901 commentary, but it was Sigmund Mowinckel who most influenced subsequent study of the book. Mowinckel maintained that the redactors of the book had before them several written sources, which they worked together to form the book of Jeremiah 1—45 (46—52 was a late appendage). Mowinckel named these sources A, B, C, and D, and he characterized them as follows:

*Source A:* found chiefly in chapters 1—23 (25); a collection of largely genuine oracles, loosely attached to each other by a redactor, without formulae of introduction or historical notice. Earlier small collections are evident within it (e.g., 21:11—22:30 on the kings), but with minor exceptions, it forms the genuine words of the prophet and is intended to give a complete collection of his preaching.

*Source B:* found chiefly in chapters 26—44. These personal-historical narratives, though not biographical in our sense of the term, are the work of an author who was interested in telling experiences of the prophet in order to provide the occasions for his memorable words. The narratives are in chronological order, with the exceptions of 26:1—27:2 and 19:1—20:6. Many scholars since have maintained rightly that Jeremiah's scribe, Baruch (cf. 36:4), was the author of this section, but Mowinckel's view was that he was an unknown scribe, a collector of popular narratives, perhaps from Egypt.

*Source C:* long speeches, belonging neither to A nor B, characteristically beginning with a superscription and sometimes a date, and having style, thought, and structure very similar to that found in Deuteronomy and the Deuteronomic history. According to Mowinckel, passages in this source included: 7:1—8:3, 11:1–5, 9–14; 18:1–12; 21:1–10; 25:1–11a; 32:1–2, 6–16, 24–44; 34:1–7, 8–22; 35:1–19; 44:1–14.

*Source D:* a small independent source found in 30:4—31:26, from an anonymous author, who collected and revised older prophecies. The source was provided by a later redactor with a Jeremianic superscription in 30:1–3 and conclusion in 31:27ff.

Since the time of Mowinckel, most scholars have recognized the same general sources, and we shall therefore use Mowinckel's nomenclature—for purpose of convenience—in our discussion.

According to Jeremiah 36, the prophet dictated all of his oracles to Baruch in 605 B.C. Since Jeremiah himself was debarred from the temple, probably because of his temple sermon (v. 5), Baruch read the scroll which contained only oracles of judgment (v. 2) before "all the people" in the temple. It is probable that the people were gathered together to hold a service of fasting and repentance on the occasion of the decisive defeat of Egypt by Babylonia at the battle of Carchemish. At any rate, the reading took place in December 604, in the temple chamber of Gemariah, who was the son of the Shaphan connected with the Deuteronomic reform in 2 Kings 22:3ff. Shaphan's grandson, Micaiah, then informed the other princes about the scroll (v. 12), among them Elnathan, also the son of a reformer (Achbor in 2 Kings 22:12–14), and Gemariah himself. The assembled princes listened to Baruch read the scroll once again (Jer. 36:15) and immediately arranged for its reading before King Jehoiakim. The king's reaction was to burn the scroll—piece by piece as it was read to him—in his stove (36:23ff.), despite the pleas of the princes that it not be burned. Yahweh therefore ordered

Jeremiah to rewrite the scroll (36:28), and Jeremiah once again dictated it to Baruch, adding to the original words of judgment "many similar words" (36:32).

Much of the scholarly work on Jeremiah has been concerned with reconstructing this original scroll, since scholars thereby hoped to regain the *ipsissima verba* of the prophet. Mowinckel maintained that his Source A contained passages of the original scroll (so too Rudolph, Bright), while others identified the original with portions of Source C (T. H. Robinson, Eissfeldt, Mohr). Other scholars made their own reconstructions (Cornill, Pfeiffer, Sellin, Hyatt), and a good deal of time and ingenuity has been poured into such effort to recover the early words of the prophet. Unfortunately, no consensus has been reached, and as Bright has pointed out, no consensus is possible. We know only that the scroll was a collection or digest of oracles dating from 627–605 B.C., that it contained oracles of judgment, and that it was short enough to be read three times in one day.

Perhaps most important for our purposes is the acceptance given the oracles of Jeremiah, according to chapter 36, by those connected to families associated with the Deuteronomic reform. We also know that other sons of the reformer Shaphan showed concern for the prophet: Ahikam saved Jeremiah's life (26:24; cf. 2 Kings 22:12, 14), and Elasah later acted as an agent for him (29:3). According to the Book of Jeremiah there is a consistent connection between Jeremiah and the reform movement.

In this connection, we therefore have to agree with Bright that Source C, which is so full of Deuteronomic language, contains authentic words and recollections of the prophet. Many scholars have argued that Source C was the product of exilic and postexilic Deuteronomists who wished to capture the sanction of Jeremiah for their own ends. Certainly C has within it many characteristic Deuteronomic phrases (for a listing, see Weinfeld), and the theology is similar to that of Deuteronomy. On the other hand, some have maintained that C was the work of Baruch. However, Holladay, in an important study in 1960, pointed out that there are phrases in C which have their prototypes in the genuine poetry of Jeremiah. Weippert recently attributed these prose speeches to the prophet himself. But it is better to understand C as the product of followers of the prophet. It embodies genuine words and recollections of the prophet, but it represents Jeremiah's preaching as it was remembered and understood by that reform group of which Jeremiah himself was a member.

Certainly the Book of Jeremiah did not take shape all at once, and there are evidences of smaller collections within the work. Chapters 1 and 25:1–13a are companion pieces, the beginning and ending of the book of oracles dating from 627–605 B.C. However, other material has been inserted into this scroll by both the prophet and others at various times. Within 1:1—25:13a smaller collections include: 2:1—4:4 on the people's sin; 4:5—6:30 and 8:14–17 on the Foe from the North; 14:1—15:4 "concerning the drought"; 21:11—23:8 to the kings of Judah; 23:9–40 "concerning the prophets." In addition, there is that large group of oracles popularly known as the Confessions of Jeremiah, which were probably never uttered publicly, but which were originally an independent collection: 11:18–23; 12:1–6; 15:10–21; 17:14–18; 18:18–23; 20:7–18.

It is difficult to read Jeremiah, because there is no clear principle of order in the book. The oracles in chapters 1—25 are in neither chronological nor topical order. The biography of chapters 26—45 is interrupted by the oracles of chapters 30—31 and 33:1—34:7. Some of the material which falls later in the book is actually very early (e.g., parts of chapters 30—31).

Some of the material has been grouped together around a common theme, as we have noted. But there are also larger complexes which apparently have been formed on the basis of common occasion or catchwords. For example, Bright points out that 18:1–12 and 19:1–13 share the catchwords "potter" and "pot." Appended to the second of these is 19:14—20:6, which shows the outcome of the pot smashing in 19:10 and which shares the catchword "Topheth" (vv. 6, 11, 13, 14). Then follows the confessional material of 20:7–18, because "terror on every side" is found in both 20:3 and 20:10. Between 18:12 and 19:1, 18:13–17 is inserted because of its theme of apostasy and because the catchword "hissed" is common to 18:16 and 19:8. Finally, 18:18–23 follows because it is similar to 20:7–18, giving a parallel form between the two sections.

Certainly some of the collections were grouped together by the prophet himself, and he may have added to his original scroll from time to time. The oral transmission of some of the oracles also has to be taken into account, although not to the extent advocated by some Scandanavian scholars in their studies of the prophets. They want to make the *writings* of the prophets wholly products of the postexilic Jewish community, with the prophetic oracles preserved only in oral form at various traditional cult-centers in the preexilic period. But one of the outstanding features of Jeremiah's activity is that he commits his oracles to writing, very likely in imitation of the written Deuteronomy. Nevertheless, some of Jeremiah's preaching also undoubtedly circulated orally, and we have to posit the most complex process in the gradual formation of his book. There were both written and oral materials, circulating both independently and in small collections, and these were gradually absorbed into larger complexes on the basis of common themes, catchwords, occasions.

In addition, there were the materials of Source C, based on the preaching of Jeremiah as his Deuteronomic followers remembered it, and this material too came into both Sources A and B. Considering the complexity of the process, it is not surprising that there are numerous doublets in the book: 6:12–15 = 8:10–12; 10:12–16 = 51:15–19; 16:14f. = 23:7f.; 23:19f. = 30:23f.; 30:10f. = 46:27f. The same material could very easily be drawn into two different complexes, in the form of both poetry and prose (e.g., 2:28 and 11:12f.; 23:5f. and 33:14–16; 31:35–37 and 33:19–26), or as both prose discourse and a part of Baruch's narrative (e.g., 7:2–15 and 26:2–6).

The Baruch biography of chapters 26—29, 32—45 (Source B) offers a wealth of detail, and despite the argument of some that the picture of Jeremiah is untrustworthy and postexilic, B has an eye-witness flavor that can only be credited to one of the prophet's intimates. The situation of 34:7 is paralleled in Lachish Letter IV:10, a detail no later writer possibly could have known, and chapter 45 could only be from Baruch himself. There is no reason for denying the source to him. C has been inserted into B at certain points, with B merely providing the framework for the prose sermons of C (e.g., 34:1–7, 8–22; 37:3–10), and thus it is reasonable to assume that B was in existence when C was written. We therefore cannot hold that C is authentic remembrance without making the same claim also for B. But again the process by which the two became fused was undoubtedly gradual and complex.

The small collection of chapters 30—31, often called "The Little Book of Comfort" (although it is not all comfort), probably assumed its present position because it served as an introduction to Jeremiah's hopeful act of the purchase of the field (chap. 32). Bright thinks chapters 32—33 may have belonged originally to the Book of Comfort. Certainly there are later additions in this source. The fall of Jerusalem is presupposed in Jeremiah 31:38-40. Hyatt would date the whole collection very late, possibly as late as Nehemiah, but most scholars consider many of the oracles to be genuine: perhaps 30:5-7, 12-17, 23-24; 31:2-6, 7-9, 10-14, 15-20, 21-22, 31-34. Some scholars would date the oracles concerning northern Israel in the early period of Jeremiah's ministry; others would place them in the time of Gedaliah, following the fall of Jerusalem.

The originally independent collection of chapters 46—51 has often been termed inauthentic. Pfeiffer and Hyatt would attribute only 46:2(3)-12 to Jeremiah, since it refers to the battle of Carchemish. Bardtke, who dated Jeremiah's call in 617 B.C., thought the oracles against the foreign nations made up Jeremiah's early preaching, and that the prophet first considered himself only a prophet to the nations. As a collection, chapters 46—51 is apparently late, but it includes much genuine material in it. Jeremiah 25:13-38 is connected with these foreign oracles; the LXX saw it as the conclusion of the collection, but most critics view it as the introduction instead. Apparently chapters 46—51 formed one of the latest additions to the Book of Jeremiah.

The final addition was the historical appendix of chapter 52. It is almost identical with 2 Kings 24:18—25:30, except for the omission of 2 Kings 25:22-26, which was already recorded more fully in Jeremiah 40:7—43:7. Jeremiah 52:28-30 is an addition from an unknown source, but apparently the redactors of Jeremiah and 2 Kings used a common source.

We can only guess how all these various collections came together to form the Book of Jeremiah as we have it. The basic Jeremianic scroll of chapters 1—25 took shape gradually, and certainly the other material was not added to it all at once. Bright has speculated that chapters 36 and 45 were first attached to the scroll, since both have to do with the occasion of its writing and form a fitting conclusion to it. Then chapters 26 and 35 were inserted before 36, since they both relate to the reign of Jehoiakim. The complex of chapters 27—29 was put after 26, because the erroneous heading in 27:1 (omitted by the LXX; RSV "Zedekiah," see margin) connects the events of chapters 27—29 with those of chapter 26, though they actually belong to 594 B.C. Chapters 30—31 early attracted 32—33, and then were prefaced with chapter 29, dealing with hope for the exiles. Chapter 34 was added because it deals with Zedekiah's reign, as do chapters 32 (v. 1) and 33 (v. 1). Finally chapters 37—44 were inserted after 36 and before 45, leaving chapter 45 as Baruch's signature. Then chapters 46—51 and 52 were appended. But this is all educated guesswork on Bright's part, and no one can be sure just how the book finally took shape. The only certainty is that the process was both gradual and complex.

One of the interesting phenomena of the book is that there are no poetic oracles from the prophet himself (with the possible exception of 30:12–17, 23–24; 31:7–9, 10–14) which date after 597 B.C. and the first Babylonian deportation. All is in prose, though certainly much is genuine. This may indicate that Jeremiah had to dictate his oracles in order for their poetic form to be preserved, that he had no opportunity to do so after 597, and that even the first person prose sections (e.g., chap. 24) come from the reform group around him. It is difficult to believe that he would otherwise deliberately so alter his style of delivery. But what this says about the collection and preservation of prophetic oracles is a subject which we cannot here pursue.

## CHAPTER EIGHT

# INVITATION AND REFUSAL

In the year that Jeremiah was called to be a prophet, Judah had become, for all practical purposes, a free country. Nabopolassar led his Babylonian forces far up the Euphrates against the weakened Assyrians and was checked in 616 B.C. only by an unusual coalition of Egypt and Assyria. In 614, the Medes under Cyaxares took the Assyrian capital of Asshur, and then in 612 combined forces with Nabopolassar to destroy Nineveh and to slay the Assyrian king (cf. Nahum). The new leader of Assyria, Ashur-uballit II, retired westward to Haran, but in 610, the Babylonians and the Medes took that city also, and when the tattered remnants of the Assyrian army, in company with Egypt, failed in 609 to retake Haran, the once mighty Assyrian Empire passed from the stage of history. It is against this background of relative freedom from foreign domination that the reform measures of Josiah and the early ministry of Jeremiah are to be understood.

No one can be absolutely sure of the dating of Jeremiah's oracles, especially since both the prophet himself (36:32) and later editors added to and revised them. But it seems probable that the following were delivered from 627–621 B.C.: 2:1–3, 20–22; 2:4–13; (perhaps 17:12–13; 16:19–21); 2:14–19, 23–28, 29–37; 3:1–5; 3:19—4:4.

Bright has stated that these early oracles are "Deuteronomic" in tone, and indeed they are. The themes are those of the reform movement. Yahweh, whose residence is in heaven (17:12; cf. 23:23; Deut. 4:36; 26:15) manifested his love for Israel in her past history. He brought Israel up out of Egypt (Jer. 2:6), led her through the terrors of the wilderness (cf. Deut. 8:15), and gave Israel the land and its "good" (Jer. 2:7; cf. Deut. 8:7–10). Israel was holy to Yahweh (Jer. 2:3; cf. Deut. 7:6; 26:19; 28:9); she was his loving bride (cf. Hos. 2:15); and therefore all who opposed her incurred guilt (2:3)—the language is cultic, reflecting Jeremiah's priestly background (cf. 2:22).

In a different figure, Israel was the son of Yahweh (3:19, 20–22; cf. 2:14, 27; 3:4), who was supposed to accept the discipline of his father (2:30; cf. Deut. 8:5). But Israel has turned to apostasy (2:5, 11, 19)—the primary sin also in Deuteronomy. He has gone after the foreign baals (2:20, 25, 27, 33; 3:1f.); he has forgotten what Yahweh has done (2:32; 3:21) and has forsaken the Lord (2:13, 19).

There is little here of the concern for social justice so prominent in the preaching of the other prophets, although Deuteronomy's concern for the poor is found in Jeremiah 2:34. Neither is there any specific punishment in view for Israel's sin.

As in Deuteronomy, Israel's apostasy has defiled Yahweh's land and made his heritage an abomination (2:7; 3:2; for the vocabulary, cf. Deut. 21:23; 24:4) by introducing into it the false gods or "abominations" of other cults (cf. Deut. 7:25f.; 12:31; 13:14; 17:1, 4; 20:18; 27:15; 32:16). The tradition about divorce at Deuteronomy 24:1–4 lies behind Jeremiah 3:1f. Similarly, the Deuteronomic traditions of the wilderness (Deut. 8:4, 15; 29:5) form the background of Jeremiah 2:25 and the prophet's continual use of the image of water (2:13, 18; cf. 2:6; 3:3; 17:5–8). It was Yahweh who gave drink in the wilderness (Deut. 8:15), and it is he who waters Palestine (Deut. 8:7; 11:14). Therefore, because Israel forsakes this fountain of living waters (Jer. 2:13), the prophet calls for the heavens to be utterly dry (2:12; RSV "desolate"), and he points out that it is the people's apostasy which has shut up the rain (3:3).

Reflecting the northern background of the reform movement, Jeremiah uses northern Israel as an example to Judah (2:4; cf. 3:6–11). It is because the northern tribes went after other gods that they became "worthless" or "empty" (*hebel*, 2 Kings 17:15), that is, they went into exile—the address to "Jacob" in 2:4 is genuine. Thus, 2:14f., 17 (v. 16 is an addition after 609 B.C.) cite the example of the North, which has become a "prey" to Assyria, as a warning to Judah (v. 18f.) to turn from apostasy.

Yahweh has an indictment or court case against Judah (2:9, 29–

37), which Jeremiah has heard in the heavenly council (see Chap. Six), and now he announces this indictment to the South. Judah is guilty of forsaking Yahweh, and now she must "return"—a constant theme of 3:1—4:4. She must remove her "abominations," that is, her foreign gods and cult practices (4:1–4). She must, as in Deuteronomy 10:16, circumcise the foreskin of her heart. Then the promise to the fathers, so prominent in Deuteronomy, will be fulfilled (Jer. 4:2). The word of God was written on Jeremiah's heart (see Chap. Six); now he issues the reform movement's call for it to be written on Judah's heart as well, so that she will love Yahweh, the only Lord, with all her heart and soul and might.

When Josiah began the expansion of his kingdom into the North, and his reform was undergirded by the finding of Deuteronomy in the temple, Jeremiah turned his attention first to the northern tribes: 3:12f.; 31:2–6, 15–20, 21f. Now there was hope for their future (31:17; cf. 29:11; 16:14f.). They had gone through the judgment which Deuteronomy warns shall fall on all apostates. They had been disciplined (31:18); they had repented (31:19). They are still Yahweh's dear son (31:20). Therefore he will have mercy on them and bring them back from captivity (31:21). He will "build" them in the land, where they shall "plant" (31:4f.; cf. 1:10) and receive the "rest" for which they once sought (31:2; cf. Deut. 28:65). Reflecting the centralization of worship in Jerusalem, they will seek God in Zion (31:6). It was the only opportunity Jeremiah had for many years to announce that Yahweh would "build" and "plant," for Judah did not take the lesson of northern Israel to "heart" (3:7–10).

Many oracles followed in this period from 622/21–609 B.C.: 11:1–5, 6–8; 18:1–12; 6:16–19, 20–21; 6:9–12; 8:4–7, 8–12; 23:9–40; 14:2–10, 11–16, 19–22; 5:20–25, 26–29, 30–31; 18:13–17; 12:1–4, 5–6; 11:18–20, 21–23; 5:1–9.

Jeremiah 11:1–5, 6–8 have been the subject of lengthy scholarly discussion. Some have claimed that "this covenant" in verse 1 refers to Josiah's covenant; others have said it means only the Sinai covenant, although of course the former was a renewal and reinterpretation of the latter. Clearly the passage belongs to the C Source, but it represents the Deuteronomic reformers' recollection of Jeremiah's preaching in support of Josiah's reform. Jeremiah 11:7f. are not in the LXX and have often been called exilic, but as in the oracles we have examined, they refer rather to the fall of the northern kingdom because of "the stubbornness of his evil heart." When Jeremiah speaks of the "fathers," he most often means Jacob and the North (cf. 34:13f. where the law of Deut. 15:1, 12 is cited). Jeremiah fully supported the Deuteronomic reform.

The incident at the potter's house in 18:1–12, then, represents the reformers' recollection of Jeremiah's proclamation of the gracious invitation of Deuteronomy: Judah has sinned, she has gone after other gods, she has passed through the awful time of apostasy under Manasseh. But Yahweh yet holds out the gracious invitation to return to him. Judah is the clay pot which has been ruined, but Yahweh can yet make of her a good vessel. The reply of the people attached to this incident (v. 12) portends the foreboding course of the future however. The people will not listen to the prophet; they will not amend their ways. Everyone will act "according to the stubbornness of his evil heart." In this period, Jeremiah becomes more and more aware of this fateful fact.

Thus, in the other oracles of this period, we find increasing evidence of Judah's rejection of Deuteronomy's grace and law. "Ask for the ancient paths," Jeremiah preaches to the people (6:16), that is, look back to the covenant instructions of Moses (cf. 18:15); then the people will find "good" and "rest." Or failing that, at least heed the sound of the war trumpet (6:17), that is, the preaching of the prophets who announce Yahweh's war (cf. Chap. Six). But the people will not give heed (6:17). They reject the *tôrāh* of Deuteronomy (6:19). They make it an object of scorn (6:10). They accept only its grace and reject its demand (8:8f., 11). They never stop to question what they are doing (8:6). They commit idolatry without giving it a second thought (8:12). This, to Jeremiah, is incomprehensible —something strange and unnatural and without precedent (8:4f., 7; 18:13f.; cf. 2:10ff.).

Jeremiah is told to search diligently among the Judeans ("the remnant of Israel," 6:9) to make sure he misses no one who will heed the word of the Lord. But the truth is that the people's ears, like their hearts, are "uncircumcised" (6:10; cf. 4:4). As a result, that "war" of Yahweh against Israel, which Jeremiah had laid on his heart in his call, will be poured out upon the whole people (6:11). Yahweh will bring the evil of punishment upon them (6:19; 8:12), but the exact nature of that punishment is still unspecified.

Apparently one of the major difficulties Jeremiah faced in his ministry was the opposition of those priests, prophets, and wise men (cf. 18:18) who continually reassured the populace that all was well. Especially the prophets gave Jeremiah trouble, for they preached "Peace, peace, when there was no peace" (8:10f.; the passage belongs here rather than in 6:13ff.). It was these false prophets of weal against which the collection of oracles in 23:9–40 (cf. 5:12f.; 14:11–16) was directed. The false prophets were preaching out of their own hearts, rather than having the word of Yahweh laid on their hearts (see Chap. Six). Apparently such prophets refused from the first to take the warning of Deuteronomy seriously, and they may have been practicing their professions in cultic centers where idolatrous practices and baal worship were carried on. The reference to "adultery" in 23:14 probably refers to their participation in, or at least support of, sacred prostitution. Thus they infected the whole land with "pollution" (23:15; RSV "ungodliness," cf. v. 10).

A remarkable judgment therefore falls on Judah, according to Jeremiah—a widespread drought (5:24; 12:4; 14:1–10; 18:13–17) —and the prophet consistently interprets this drought as Deuteronomy's "curse" against apostasy. It is because the land is full of "polluters" that the pastures are dried up (23:10). It is because the people have a stubborn and rebellious heart (5:23), because they do not fear or obey Yahweh (5:24), the giver of the rain in its season (Deut. 11:14; 28:12), because they have eyes but see not, and ears but hear not (Deut. 29:4). Their sin has kept the "good" of the watered land from them (Jer. 5:25). It is absolutely inconceivable that Yahweh, the fountain of living waters (2:13) should run dry— such is the meaning implied in 18:14. But the people have forgotten Yahweh and burned incense to false gods and turned aside from the ancient way (18:15). Therefore the drought has come upon them. The people have had other gods before Yahweh's face (Deut. 5:7); therefore Yahweh has hid his face from them (Jer. 18:17; cf. 2:27; Deut. 31:17f.; 32:20). Even passersby realize that the drought is Yahweh's judgment upon his people (Jer. 18:16).

Jeremiah's preaching of this judgment led to early opposition to him on the part of religious leaders even within his own territory of Benjamin and within his own hometown and circle of kin. The prophet raised a complaint to the Lord about this opposition (12:1f.). Yahweh's answer to this lawsuit was that the opposition was only beginning (12:5f.). Nevertheless, he promised punishment of Jeremiah's persecutors (11:21f.), and Jeremiah, secure in the knowledge of his call and in Yahweh's judgment by drought, rested his case in Yahweh's hands (11:20). He was at this time forced to move to Jerusalem, however.

What Jeremiah saw in Jerusalem did not reassure him. He was commanded by Yahweh to search that city for just one person who was faithful to the *tôrāh* of Yahweh (5:4f.). But he found no one, either among the poor or among the landed leaders, who would accept the discipline of the Lord and repent (5:3). As in Deuteronomy 8:11ff., the people ate and were full (cf. Jer. 5:27f.), and then went trooping after the baals, participating in the rites of sacred prostitution. They oppressed the orphans and needy in the courts (5:28), probably for the sake of bribes (cf. Deut. 16:18ff.), and hence grew rich (5:27). "Shall I not punish them for these things," Yahweh asked, "and shall I not avenge myself on a nation such as this" (5:9, 29; cf. 9:9)? It was becoming clear that the Deuteronomic reform was really not reforming the people's hearts.

The reform cause certainly was not aided by the death of its instigator, Josiah. When the Egyptians under Neco II (609–593 B.C.) marched north in 609 to aid the Assyrian effort to retake Haran, Josiah tried to stop them at Megiddo. He was mortally wounded in battle and dead by the time he was returned to Jerusalem (2 Chron. 35:20–25). His son Jehoahaz (Shallum) reigned only three months and then was deposed by Neco and deported to Egypt (cf. Jer. 22:10ff.). Jehoahaz' brother Eliakim was placed on the throne as an Egyptian vassal, his name changed to Jehoiakim, and Judah laid under heavy tribute. The brief time of independence was at an end. Such a change of fortune must have spelled the final abandonment of reform efforts on the part of the populace (cf. Jer. 44:17f.).

To make matters worse, Jehoiakim was a despot. He was placed on the throne by a foreign power and thus had no covenant with the people or Yahweh. He murdered a prophet named Uriah, who opposed him (Jer. 26:20–23). Then, despite the heavy taxation laid on the people to pay off Neco (2 Kings 23:35), he decided to renovate his palace, so that he might have a window where he could appear before the people (such is the meaning of Jer. 22:14), and decorated it after the manner of Egyptian palaces. To accomplish this building project, he pressed his free countrymen into the hated corvée or forced labor (22:13), evidently enforcing his policies with the sword (22:17). Jeremiah was now confronted with his major enemy.

The attitude of the prophet toward the monarchy is clearly set out in principle in 21:11f. and 22:1–5, 6f.: the Judean kings were subject to the covenant of Deuteronomy and responsible for the maintenance of justice and the protection of the weak within society. They had no more status before Yahweh than did the ordinary Israelite (cf. "neighbor," 22:13). If they fulfilled the *tôrāh* by doing justice and maintaining righteousness from their "heart" (22:17), then they received "good" from Yahweh (22:15f.; RSV "well"). Because Jehoiakim violated these covenant demands, Jeremiah prophesied for him a violent and unmourned death (in contrast to the lamentation over Josiah, 22:10), a prophecy which apparently never was fulfilled (cf. 2 Kings 24:6; 2 Chron. 36:8).

It must be realized that in turning against the Davidic king, Jeremiah was attacking the center of Judean stability, with its foundation in the promise of Yahweh to the house of David. In 608 B.C., the prophet widened this attack by leveling Yahweh's judgment against the temple worship also (7:1–15; 26:1–6). In Davidic king and temple, with its ark, symbolizing the presence of Yahweh in her midst, Judah rested all her hope, and not without earlier prophetic warrant. A century earlier Isaiah had proclaimed that Zion was invincible, and that the Davidic king should put all his trust in the promise to David (cf. Isa. 7). But under Jehoiakim, temple worship came to be understood as a magical guarantee of Yahweh's protection (Jer. 7:4). Foreign gods were again set up in the temple itself (7:30), the abominable practice of child sacrifice was reintroduced (7:31), worship of the astral bodies was resumed (7:18), and the stipulations of the Decalogue were systematically broken (7:9; cf. Hos. 4:2). Yet the people came into the temple and assured themselves that Yahweh looked in favor upon them (7:10). The temple had become for them "a den of robbers" (7:11), that is, a hiding place (cf. Mark 11:17 and pars.). In his temple sermon, Jeremiah therefore proclaimed that the temple would be destroyed, as the amphictyonic center at Shiloh had been destroyed by the Philistines about the year 1050 B.C. (7:12, 14), and that the Judeans would go into exile, as the inhabitants of the northern kingdom had gone (7:15).

The C version of the temple sermon, in 7:1–7, seems to indicate that Jeremiah's preaching on this occasion was conditional: *if* the people would amend their ways, they would be allowed to remain in the land. But the rest of the sermon, in 7:8ff., and the reaction to it recorded by Baruch, in 26:7ff., indicate that Jeremiah's pronouncement was absolute: temple and city would become desolate without inhabitant (26:9).

The reaction of the priests and prophets to Jeremiah's words was immediate. The nobles were summoned to the temple gate, and Jeremiah was tried on the spot. Priests and prophets demanded a sentence of death (26:10f.). Jeremiah's defense was that he was truly speaking Yahweh's word, and that his death would bring God's retaliation ("innocent blood," cf. Deut. 21:8). Appealing to oral prophetic tradition in the community, the elders, nobles, and people took Jeremiah's side (26:16–19), and finally the appeal of Ahikam, a reformer's son, saved the prophet's life (26:24). Jeremiah now had the monarchy and the cultic leaders against him, however, and he was henceforth debarred from entering the temple.

It had become clear in this period of 609–605 B.C. that the effects of the Deuteronomic reform were gone forever. The people and their leaders would not circumcize their hearts and return to the Lord. They would not accept Deuteronomy's gracious invitation to life and good. The inevitable result, as Deuteronomy had said, was that judgment and evil would come upon them, as Yahweh poured out his wrath upon their idolatrous ways.

This state of affairs is vividly pictured in the lament of Yahweh in 9:2–9. The Lord speaks throughout the poem, and he says that the Judeans are all "adulterers," that is, worshipers of other gods (v. 2). They are all deceivers and supplanters like Jacob (cf. Gen. 25:26), the symbol of the unfaithful northern kingdom. Their society is full of lies and cheating, falsehoods and broken covenants. The intimate relation to Yahweh has been lost completely, so that ethical living among neighbors and families has become impossible. The reaction of Yahweh is utter weariness and grief: he would just like to rent a room out in the desert and get away from them all. But he has not given up completely. He will still try to refine the people in the fires of his judgment (v. 7). He has not yet removed all grace from them. It is an indication of the patience and yearning mercy of God that he has not yet finally rejected such a society. Perhaps there is hope for our own communities, so full of broken family and societal covenants, so distorted with leaders' propaganda and the devaluation of language, so complacent about religion's use as a magical guarantee of God's favor. Perhaps. But as we shall see, God's patience with Judah does not endure forever.

## CHAPTER NINE

# JUDGMENT AND CONFESSION

"Surely the Lord God does nothing, without revealing his secret to his servants the prophets" (Amos 3:7). It was in this critical period of 609–605 B.C. that Yahweh revealed to Jeremiah that he was bringing judgment out of the north upon Judah. In an ecstatic vision, Jeremiah saw a pot, its fire being fanned, its evil brew spilling out toward the south (Jer. 1:13–19). Yahweh was calling "the kingdoms of the north" to war against Judah, and they would besiege Jerusalem and bring the verdict of Yahweh's court against her (v. 15f.). Jeremiah was to "gird up his loins" for the action of war, and once again he was reassured that the whole land would fight against him, but that Yahweh was with him in the war to deliver him (v. 17ff.).

Following this "second" call (cf. v. 13; 11:9–17), the prophet therefore delivered a series of oracles on the Foe from the North: 4:5–8, 13–18, 19–22, 29–31; 5:15–17; 6:1–8, 22–26; 8:14–16. No collection in the book has occasioned more scholarly discussion, with regard to the identity of the Foe and therefore to the dating of Jeremiah's ministry. Early commentators identified the Foe with an invasion of barbarian Scythians from the Caucasus in 626 B.C., but such identification is based on Herodotus' questionable accounts and has been largely discarded. Some have pointed to the Medes, others to the Babylonians. Welch maintained that the Foe was not a specific nation, but symbolic of the coming Day of the Lord, with the figures of the "North" and of the "lion destroyer" taken from Near Eastern mythology. Staerk attributed the Foe to an ancient myth of the destruction of the world. Childs has shown, however, that the Foe has a historical and not a mythological character, and there now seems to be an emerging consensus among scholars that Jeremiah is speaking of historical enemies, but that initially he has no specific

73

nations in mind. The figure of the "North" is borrowed from Canaan-ite mythology, in which the mountain of the gods is located "in the far north" (cf. Ps. 48:2; Isa. 14:13). Thus the destruction comes from Yahweh, in the form of an unknown enemy (cf. Amos 3:6). Jeremiah is commanded to announce such coming judgment, and he faithfully does so. It is not until a later time that the Foe is explicitly revealed to be the Babylonians.

The description which Jeremiah gives of the coming Foe is terri-fying (cf. Jer. 6:25; 8:15). The attacking nations are described as "a lion" (4:7; cf. 5:6; Amos 3:4, 8, 12; Hos. 11:10), "a destroyer of nations" (4:7), whose "chariots are like the whirlwind" (4:13; cf. v. 11), whose "horses are swifter than eagles" (4:13; cf. v. 29; 6:23; 8:16; Deut. 28:49). They are a "nation from afar," "an en-during nation," "an ancient nation," "whose language you do not know" (5:15; cf. Deut. 28:49). They use the bow and spear (4:29; 5:16; 6:23), and attack in battle formation (6:23). They are "cruel and have no mercy" (6:23), besieging cities (4:16; 6:6), and reduc-ing them to ruins (4:7, 13; 5:17; 6:5; 8:14; cf. Deut. 28:52) with-out inhabitant (4:7, 29; cf. 9:11; 10:22; 4:25f.).

Therefore Judah is called to don sackcloth and to enter into lamentation (4:8; 6:26). The war standard will be raised and the trumpet will sound throughout the land (4:5f., 19, 21; 6:1), because Yahweh's fierce anger has not turned back (4:8). The people are stupid, with no understanding, skilled in doing evil (4:22), keeping their wickedness always fresh (6:7), and refusing to cleanse their "hearts" (4:14). Therefore their doom shall reach their "hearts" (4:18), for suddenly the destroyer shall come upon them (6:26). In prophetic vision, the prophet sees the whole land and his own camp laid waste (4:19–22).

It was the awful burden of Jeremiah that he was a messenger called to proclaim a divine war against his people which he himself never wanted, and there is evidence in his writings that he resisted the word of war laid upon his heart with all the strength of his being. Once he tried to shut it up within himself and not proclaim it (20:9). Other times he pushed the prophetic function of intercession before God on behalf of the people to its ultimate limits: he pleaded with Yahweh to turn aside from wrath and to bring "good" on the people instead

(18:20). He never desired the "day of disaster" for his people (17:16), and he was horror struck by the visions of ruin which he saw and heard, in prophetic ecstasy, to be coming upon his countrymen (4:19–21; cf. 4:23–26?). In one of the most moving elegies of the book (8:18—9:1), probably to be dated shortly before 597, he grieves, heartsick over the fact that Judah cannot be saved. There is "no balm in Gilead to heal the sin-sick soul," and Jeremiah wishes his head were water and his eyes a fountain of tears, that he might weep day and night for those of his compatriots who will be slain in the coming destruction (cf. Rom. 9:1ff.).

So deep is Jeremiah's grief for his people that he apparently continually barrages Yahweh with pleas to save them (cf. Luke 11:5–13; 18:1–8). The result is that the Lord must finally tell him to be silent (Jer. 7:16; 11:14; 14:11). More than that, Yahweh must time and again explain to the prophet why it is absolutely necessary that the people be punished (7:17ff.; 11:15; cf. 5:9, 29; 9:9), and we have the astounding picture of the Lord of Israel justifying his actions to his messenger (7:19). The explanation is that the people have so rebelled against God in their apostasy that even the intercession of Moses and Samuel would not be sufficient to save them (15:1–3).

Judah's sin is written with a "pen of iron; with a point of diamond it is engraved on the tablet of their heart" (17:1)—that is the major indictment of Yahweh against his people in the Book of Jeremiah. If we recall that the words of Deuteronomy were to be on Israel's heart (Deut. 6:6) and taught to her children (6:7), then the meaning of 17:1–4 becomes quite clear, despite the corrupt nature of the Hebrew text. Judah has not taken Yahweh's *tôrāh* to heart, but instead has turned aside to worship other gods and has taught her children to go after the fertility gods, in total violation of Deuteronomy's law. The reform measures have been left behind; apostasy is rife throughout the country. The result is that Judah will become the "spoil" of Yahweh's war (Jer. 17:3) and lose her good land or heritage, in fulfillment of the Deuteronomic curse.

It should be noted in this connection that Yahweh's anger against his people is pictured in terms of a "fire" (17:4; the verse belongs here, not in 15:13f.). This is the symbol used consistently of

Yahweh's judgment throughout the Book of Jeremiah (4:4; 11:16; 17:27; 21:14; 22:7), most often in passages attributed to the C Source. But those passages reflect the preaching of the prophet himself, for the word on his heart and in his mouth is a word of "fire" (5:14; 20:9; 23:29), which tests and assays and attempts to refine the people, but all in vain (6:27–30). Therefore the judgment of "fire" breaks forth, and significant in this connection is that in Deuteronomy, Yahweh is a devouring fire (4:24) in his acts of Holy War (9:3). The fire of judgment which is loosed by Jeremiah's word on Judah is the fire of Yahweh's war against her.

Such was the burden of the message which the prophet dictated to Baruch the scribe and which was read before King Jehoiakim in December 604 B.C. (cf. 45:1–5; note the "war" of v. 5). It is an ironic twist in the story that Jehoiakim tried to get rid of the fiery war of judgment pronounced on Judah by burning the pieces of the prophetic scroll in his little warming brazier (36:22f.)!

It was clear by that time that any Foe from the North would be the Babylonians (36:29). From 609–605 B.C., Judah was an Egyptian vassal. But in 605, Nebuchadnezzar of Babylonia delivered a crushing defeat to the Egyptians at Carchemish and Hamath (46:3–12, 14–24), and the way lay open to him into Syria and Palestine. In August of 605, upon the death of Nabopolassar, Nebuchadnezzar had to return home to assume the throne, but by the end of 604, he was once again in the Philistine plain (47:2–7), where he destroyed Ashkelon and deported some of its leaders to Babylon. By 603/2, Jehoiakim had become his vassal (2 Kings 24:1).

Jehoiakim apparently did not believe, however, that the Babylonians would attack his kingdom, and so his reaction to Jeremiah's word of war was scornful rejection. Moreover, from 604–601 B.C., Babylonia did not attack, and it was this circumstance which gave rise to many of those individual laments and complaints by Jeremiah which are known popularly as his Confessions (15:10f., 15–18, 19–21; 17:14–18; 18:19–23; 20:7–13, 14–18; we have dealt previously with 11:18–20, 21–23; 12:1–6).

During this period, Jeremiah pronounced only woe upon his sinful people (13:20–27): they could not do "good" any more than the Ethiopian could change his skin or the leopard his spots (v. 23).

They never turned aside from their apostasy (v. 27), to the utter grief of the prophet (13:17). Their reaction to his words was like the careless revelry of a bunch of drunkards (13:12)—the people laughed as Jeremiah wept for the ruin that was coming upon them.

In fact in this period, Yahweh commanded Jeremiah to become a living symbol of the divine rejection of Judah (16:1–13). The prophet had early in his career been forbidden to marry (v. 1f.). We must assume the actual command followed shortly after his call, since Israelite youths married at an early age. But now the reason for this divine command was made clear: the merriment of weddings, the immortality given a man in the perpetuation of his name in his off-spring, the future granted through the inheritance of children, were to be lost to Judah (16:3f., 9; cf. 7:34; 25:10). Jeremiah's single isolation was a symbol of that fact. Moreover, Jeremiah was forbidden to go either to a party (16:8; cf. 15:17) or to a funeral (16:5ff.), for the fellowship both of celebration and of mourning would be lost to Judah. The view of the funeral and grief here is that the ability of a people to mourn together is also a gift of God's grace. Jeremiah personally becomes the symbol of Yahweh's withdrawal of all grace from Judah. According to verse 5, God has taken away his *šālôm* or peace, his *hesed* or covenant love, and his *rah̬ᵃmîm* or tender mercy (cf. 8:13). Jeremiah's utter isolation from human companionship is living symbol of that fact (cf. 15:17).

So Jeremiah preached, but for several years no enemy, no divine judgment came upon his country. The result was that Jeremiah became a laughingstock to his compatriots. "Where is the word of the Lord?" his colleagues hooted. "Let it come!" (17:15). After one preaching incident (19:14f.), Pashhur the priest even put the prophet in the stocks overnight, where Jeremiah could be derided and mocked by passersby (20:1f., cf. v. 8). The mocking taunted Jeremiah with his own words of doom, "Terror on every side" (20:10; cf. 6:25; 46:5). Thus his preaching was turned into a joke, and the prophet was forced to suffer his deepest humiliation (cf. "shame," 17:18; "reproach and derision," 20:8).

Those who are publicly humiliated, however, are soon bodily threatened, and the laughter against Jeremiah turned into hatred (15:10) and actual threats against his life (18:18, 20, 22; 20:10).

Apparently the hope of his opponents was to denounce him as a false prophet and thereby to bring on him the legal punishment of stoning (20:10).

That Jeremiah was terror stricken is understandable (cf. 17:17). He was almost totally alone, his isolation broken only by the occasional company of Baruch, who had his own problems (cf. 45:2f.). The company of Yahweh with Jeremiah was that of a "dread warrior" (20:11), the content of his word that of "violence," "destruction" (20:8), and the divine "indignation" (15:17). It was not a happy message to preach day in and day out, though apparently the prophet found occasional joy in his endeavors (15:16). But the fact that Yahweh's word did not come to pass led the prophet into reactions alien to him: he prayed that Yahweh would fulfill his word of judgment upon the people (17:18; cf. 18:21f.) and thus vindicate his preaching and his ministry (20:12).

Initially Jeremiah never doubted that such would be the case (20:11–13). He knew that his words had come from the Lord in his heavenly council (cf. 17:16de). As time passed and the word was not fulfilled, however, the prophet turned first against Yahweh's purpose for his life (20:14–18) and then against Yahweh himself. Since he had been set aside to be a prophet even before his birth (1:5), Jeremiah therefore cursed the day of his birth and the innocent neighbor who had announced his birth (20:14ff.). He wished the day were blotted out from time, and the neighbor destroyed like Sodom and Gomorrah because he did not kill Jeremiah in the womb. It was a totally irrational wish, but a measure of the prophet's desperation. In 20:14–18, Jeremiah rejects God's total purpose for his life. Verse 18 reads: "Why this? From the womb I came forth to see misery and grief, and my days are consumed in shame." There is not a ray of light that illumines the darkness of the prophet's ministry.

But Jeremiah's despair grows darker still. In the last of his laments, 15:15–18, he turns to, and then finally against, the God who has called him. He is afraid Yahweh has forgotten him (v. 15b), that the Lord will forever show forbearance toward his sinful people and never bring the promised judgment upon them (v. 15d), that therefore his pain will be unceasing and his only ending death (v. 18abc). If that happens, then Yahweh, the fountain of living waters (2:13), the never-ending stream (cf. 18:14), will have become as inconstant as a desert wadi which one minute gushes with water and the next runs dry (v. 18de). Jeremiah always felt that Yahweh had lured him into the ministry against his will (20:7; "deceived" has the meaning of "seduce" or "lure"; see Exod. 22:16; Judg. 16:5; 1 Kings 22: 20ff.). Now in this lament, Jeremiah accuses God of doing so deceitfully, of putting a word on his heart (15:16) which would never be fulfilled (v. 18). The prophet's suffering has led him to lose his faith and to blaspheme his God.

In the usual structure of an individual lament, the petition for relief is often followed by an expression of certainty or trust, which was a response to an intervening priestly oracle of salvation (cf. 20:13; Ps. 6:8–10). Jeremiah 15:19–21 takes the place of the priestly oracle, but the words are by no means only reassuring. Rather, in stunning similarity to Jeremiah's early admonitions to his people that they "return" to the fountain of living waters, the prophet himself is told by God to return. Jeremiah must recover his faith in Yahweh's word. He has almost forfeited his ministry by doubting the efficacy of Yahweh's word, and only if he trusts that word once more will he continue to be allowed in Yahweh's council (v. 19). There is an intimation that the word will come to pass and that the people will then seek out Jeremiah, but Jeremiah's isolation will remain: he is not to turn to the people. He will always have to stand over against them as the messenger of Yahweh's council. Nevertheless, he is promised that he will escape with his life. The assurance of his initial call, that Yahweh is with him to deliver him, is renewed (v. 20f.).

So the prophet is to have no relief from the strife that consumes his days; that is true of Jeremiah's ministry to the very end. Until the close of his life, Jeremiah is a man of suffering and acquainted with grief. But after this rebuke by Yahweh, the prophet went on with his preaching, and the fact that he did so is evidence of his renewed trust in his Lord. Indeed, the fact that he later wrote down his *Confessions* is evidence of that trust, for had he never recovered his faith, he could not have confessed so clearly the difference between his own sinful ways and the purposes of his God. Neither could he have shown us so forcefully what it means to wrestle in prayer with the demands of the living God.

The God of the Bible is faithful to his word (cf. Isa. 40:8; 55:10f.; Matt. 24:35). He always keeps his promises. The announced war against Judah therefore finally came. In 601, Nebuchadnezzar's army was battered in a battle with the Egyptian forces of Neco, and the Babylonian ruler returned home to recoup his losses. Seeing his opportunity, Jehoiakim rebelled (2 Kings 24:1), but it was a foolhardy venture. Though Nebuchadnezzar was elsewhere occupied, he dispatched allied guerrilla bands and Babylonian shock troops against the Judean kingdom (2 Kings 24:2; Jer. 35:11). To Jeremiah, it was a clear intimation of the end, and the oracle he pronounced at the time is chilling in its implications (12:7–13). Yahweh had now forsaken Judah. His love for her hand turned into hatred (v. 8). Judah well might have asked, "If God be against us, who can be for us?" (*contra* Rom. 8:31). When God hates a people, they literally have no future and no hope of life.

In December of 598, Nebuchadnezzar himself marched against Jerusalem. In the same month, Jehoiakim died and was succeeded by his eighteen-year-old son Jehoiachin (Coniah) (2 Kings 24:8; Jer. 22:20–23, 24–27). After a brief siege (Jer. 10:17f.), Jerusalem surrendered, the temple was despoiled, an enormous booty was taken, and Jehoiachin himself, along with his mother (cf. 13:18f.), the reigning nobles, the artisans, and the warriors were carried into Babylonian exile (22:28ff.). Judah's territory was greatly reduced, and she was left virtually without economic means and political leadership (10:19–21). Jeremiah called for the professional women mourners to raise their dirge over the city (9:17–22): "Death has come up into our windows." The word of Yahweh's war against Judah had begun to come to pass.

## CHAPTER TEN

# A FUTURE AND A HOPE

On the throne of Judah, Nebuchadnezzar placed Zedekiah (Mattaniah), the twenty-one-year-old uncle of the deposed Jehoiachin. In more tranquil days, Zedekiah might have proved a mild and beneficent ruler, but his position was too ambiguous and his will too weak to withstand the storms that raged about Judah at the beginning of the sixth century B.C. Zedekiah was surrounded by an inexperienced court, some favoring Babylonia, most looking to Egypt for an opportunity to revolt. Many Judeans still regarded the exiled Jehoiachin as the legitimate king. Among those Jews carried into exile were a number of prophets who constantly fanned the flames of rebellion (29:8f., 21ff.), and in Jerusalem, other prophets predicted a swift end to the Babylonian rule (chap. 28).

Perhaps also encouraged by the accession of Psammetichus II in Egypt, a number of ambassadors from the small western states met in Jerusalem in 594/93 to plot revolt against their Babylonian masters (27:3). Apparently nothing came of their intrigue. Certainly Jeremiah opposed it (chaps. 27—28), and Egypt did not support it. Zedekiah therefore felt constrained first to send a deputation (29:3) and then personally to go to Babylon (51:59) to reassure Nebuchadnezzar of Judah's continuing loyalty.

Jeremiah made several unique pronouncements during this period from 597–593 B.C. Immediately after the deportation of 597 and for the first time since the early days of his ministry, he was able to announce the comforting word that Yahweh was not only plucking up and breaking down (1:10), but also building and planting (24:1–7, v. 6). The hope for Judah's future, he said, lay with those who had already gone through the fire of Yahweh's judgment. The deportees of 597 were the "good figs" (cf. Amos 8:1–3). Now Yahweh would set his eyes upon them for "good" and bring them back to the land. He would give them a "heart" to know his lordship, so they would return to their covenant relationship with him "with their whole heart" (v. 7; cf. Deut. 30:6). Jeremiah's preaching of salvation was framed in Deuteronomy's motifs.

Further, it was to Deuteronomy's law that Jeremiah looked in the contest with the prophet Hananiah (chap. 28). Jeremiah donned a wooden yoke (27:2) as prophetic symbol of the fact that Yahweh, the Lord of all the earth (v. 5), had given the lands of the Palestinian land-bridge into the hand of Nebuchadnezzar. This occupation would continue until such time as Yahweh himself would bring Nebuchadnezzar's house to an end (27:6f.; Nebuchadnezzar's line actually ended in 560 B.C. though the Babylonian captivity did last almost 70 years). The other (cultic?) prophets opposed Jeremiah's word, assuring the people that Babylonia's power would soon be broken and that the exiles and the temple furnishings would be returned speedily. Hananiah even put a figure on it: two years (28:3). Jeremiah had no immediate word from the Lord to answer (28:5f.), relying instead on prophetic tradition (28:8) and Deuteronomy's test of prophecy (28:9; Deut. 18:21f.). But when the word did come to Jeremiah, it was very clear: Babylonia's yoke would not be removed; Hananiah was a false prophet and would die (28:15f.; Deut. 13:5), a prediction which soon came to pass (Jer. 28:17).

Moreover, Jeremiah wrote a letter to the exiles in Babylonia (29:4–15, 21–23; vv. 16–20 are extraneous insert), urging them to "build" houses and to "plant" gardens in Babylonia, to intermarry with their captors (v. 5f.), and even to pray for Babylonia's welfare (v. 7; for "city" read "country"). On the face of it, Jeremiah was urging treason, but he wrote what he did because the word of the Lord clearly indicated that Judah was to live in captivity until the seventy years of Babylonia's rule were past. Then and only then would Yahweh bring Judah back to Palestine (29:10f.; cf. 50:1— 51:58; 51:59–62). Yahweh's war against Judah would come to an end and then he would bring *šālôm* upon her. She had "a future and a hope," but only in God's time and God's purpose, after she had passed through judgment (29:11). Then the word of Deuteronomy 4:29 would be fulfilled: Judah would seek Yahweh and he would be found by her and brought back from exile (Jer. 29:12–14).

The result of Jeremiah's letter was that Shemaiah, a priest among the exiles, wrote the priest Zephaniah in Jerusalem, urging him to silence the "madman" Jeremiah (v. 24ff.). Whether in friendship or warning, Zephaniah read the letter to Jeremiah, who promptly proclaimed Yahweh's word that Shemaiah and his family would not live to see the "good" which Yahweh would do in the future (v. 32).

As always, Judah did not heed Jeremiah's word. By 589, open rebellion had broken out, and in January 588, the Babylonians placed Jerusalem under blockade.

At this time, there began a series of dialogues between Jeremiah and the terrified King Zedekiah. The latter sent a deputation to the prophet, urging his intercession, in the hope that Yahweh would deliver them by one of his "wonderful deeds," as he had done in the time of Hezekiah (21:1f.; cf. 2 Kings 18:17—19:37 = Isa. 36—37). Jeremiah's reply was that this was Yahweh's war against Judah, that many would die, and that Zedekiah and the survivors would be given into the hand of Nebuchadnezzar (21:5ff.).

At the same time, in a remarkable reinterpretation of Deuteronomy 30:15, Jeremiah set before the people "the way of life and the way of death" (21:8ff.)—either surrender to the Babylonians or die, for Yahweh's face was against Jerusalem for evil and not for "good." The description of the judgment in this period is, repeatedly, that the city shall be burned with "fire" (cf. 34:2, 22; 38:17, etc.): the phrase is symbolic of that Holy War of the God who comes as a "devouring fire" (see Chap. Nine).

Jeremiah followed this warning with a personal oracle to Zedekiah (34:2–5): the city would be put to the torch and Zedekiah would see Nebuchadnezzar face to face. But if the king submitted to Babylonia, he would live and have a peaceful and honorable death.

Perhaps by the summer of 588, Jerusalem's outlying defenses had been broken. Nebuchadnezzar now lay siege to the city itself. In a panic of desperation-religion, Zedekiah and the people decided that perhaps their hope lay in obedience to the Deuteronomic *tôrāh* after all. They therefore held a covenant renewal ceremony, and as a sign of their good faith, proclaimed the year of release for Hebrew slaves, stipulated in the law of Deuteronomy 15:1, 12–18 (Jer. 34:8–10; cf. v. 16 with Deut. 21:14). Amazingly, news arrived of an approaching Egyptian force, and the Babylonians were forced temporarily to lift the siege. One would think that the Judeans would view such an event as evidence of the divine favor toward their new-found obedience. Instead, in their superficial piety, they immediately forgot about the covenant renewal and took back the slaves (vv. 11–16). Yahweh's reaction was renewed judgment upon the covenant transgressors (vv. 17–22). The Babylonians would return—which they soon did—and the city would be burned with "fire" (v. 22; 37:3–10).

Sometime during the break in the siege, however, Jeremiah attempted to go to Benjamin to attend to some family property matters (perhaps the same as those in 32:6ff.). He was accused of desertion, not without some reason (cf. 21:9; 38:19), arrested, beaten by members of the palace court and imprisoned in a dungeon in the house of Jonathan, where he surely would have died (37:11–16).

Bright believes we have parallel accounts in 37:11–21 and 38:1–28a (cf. also Skinner), but much evidence argues against the conclusion. It accords with the uncertain character of Zedekiah that he would have repeatedly turned to the prophet for a word from Yahweh (37:17–21; 38:14–26). There are no details in the stories which prevent them from being read as consecutive actual accounts. Bright interprets 52:6f. as meaning that Jerusalem's food supply lasted until the city fell (cf. 37:21). However, we know that the inhabitants were even forced to cannabalism in the final days of the siege (see Ezek. 5:10; Jer. 19:9 and Lam. 2:12, 19–20; 4:4, 7–10). Thus there could have been some days' time between Jeremiah 37:21 and 38:28.

Jeremiah was saved from death in the dungeon only because the fearful Zedekiah sent for him secretly to inquire of the Lord (37:17). Jeremiah gave Zedekiah no hope, but he did point out the falsity of the other prophetic counsel which Zedekiah had been receiving. He also won the right to be imprisoned in the court of the guard which was adjacent to the palace and which allowed Jeremiah a certain measure of freedom (37:18–21). Jeremiah used the opportunity to continue to counsel passersby to surrender (38:4). As a result, the weak Zedekiah surrendered Jeremiah's fate to court officials, who lowered the prophet into a muddy cistern and left him to die of thirst or suffocation in the mire (38:5f.). A court eunuch, however, interceded with the wishy-washy Zedekiah and restored the prophet to the guard court (38:7–13; cf. 39:15–18). Once again Zedekiah secretly sought a word from Jeremiah, and revealed that he hesitated to surrender because he feared the Jews who had deserted to the Babylonians would abuse him if he fell into their hands (38:14–19). Jeremiah tried to reassure the monarch (38:20) and lied to save him (38:27). But he could not alter Yahweh's judgment.

In July 587, Jerusalem's walls were breached by the Babylonians. Zedekiah and some of his troops fled by night toward Ammon, but were overtaken near Jericho and hauled before Nebuchadnezzar at Riblah in central Syria. Zedekiah's sons were executed, and he himself was blinded and deported in chains to Babylonia (39:1–2, 4–8; cf. 52:4–16). (Note the fulfillment of Jer. 1:15f. in 39:3.) A month later, the Babylonian commander Nebuzaradan arrived at Jerusalem, leveled its walls, put its buildings to the torch, led many of its officials to be executed at Riblah (52:24–27), and then carried into Babylonian exile all but the poorest peasants (39:10). The word of Yahweh's war had now spent itself on Judah. That nation had been put to death by the Lord over life and death. But always that Lord weeps over the refusal of his sinful people to return to him: "O Jerusalem, Jerusalem, killing the prophets and stoning those who are sent to you! (Matt. 23:37f. and par.).

It is the nature of the word of God in the Bible, however, that precisely in the midst of death, it nevertheless proclaims life. It was while Jerusalem was still under siege and Jeremiah was imprisoned in the court of the guard that the word of the Lord came to him, commanding him to redeem a piece of family property which had fallen to him at Anathoth (32:1–17a, 24–27, 36–44). In strict legal fashion (cf. Lev. 25:25), Jeremiah purchased the land, as a prophetic symbolic act that "houses and fields and vineyards shall again be bought in this land" (v. 15). While Jerusalem was falling, Yahweh promised that it would be restored! The word of judgment was not the final word. Rather, as in Deuteronomy 30:1–8, Yahweh would gather his people from their places of exile, bring them back to Palestine, and restore his covenant with them. He would give them a new "heart," so that they would obey him, and he would do them "good," planting them once more in their land.

It may also have been at this time that the oracles of 30:5–7, 10–11, 12–17; 31:7–9, 10–14, with their promises of restoration, were uttered. The first two reflect the judgment on Judah followed by her restoration. The latter two are directed to the North, which has already passed through its time of judgment. Many have attributed these latter to a later hand, on the basis of their similarities to Second Isaiah, but they reflect many of Jeremiah's themes: note especially Ephraim, the first-born son of Yahweh, the emphasis on "good," the water and fructility of the land restored, the transformation of mourning into merrymaking (31:9, 12–14).

It is also possible that 30:18–21; 31:35–37 and 23:5–6 (cf. 33:14–16) belong in this period, though their genuineness has often been questioned. We do not know for certain whether Jeremiah ever envisioned the restoration of the Davidic kingship, but since 23:5–6 and 33:14–16 were both preserved, it is possible that he did. ("The Lord is our righteousness" is a wordplay on the name of Zedekiah). Certainly his vision of the righteous king was of a ruler once more obedient to the *tôrāh* of Deuteronomy (cf. Deut. 6:25).

In his prophecies of the future, Jeremiah was sure of one fact: only Yahweh could restore Israel to wholeness and faithfulness. For thirty-eight years, the prophet had preached and pleaded with his apostate people to circumcise the foreskin of their hearts. Only so could they receive the word of the Deuteronomic covenant in faith and gratitude and their lives reflect their obedience and knowledge and love of their divine Father and Redeemer (cf. Ezek. 18:30–32). But Israel would not listen (cf. Zech. 7:12). She ignored God's prophet, mocked him, drove him out of his hometown, threatened him, and finally tried several times to kill him. If there was healing for such a people, it would have to come from Yahweh himself. Israel had no power within herself to amend her ways and transform her own sinful heart (cf. Hos. 5:4). If the Ethiopian could change his skin or the leopard his spots, then also Israel, who was accustomed to doing evil, could do good (Jer. 13:23). The sin of Israel was written with the point of a diamond upon the tablet of her heart, and there was nothing Israel could do to expunge that sin (17:1).

Israel had to be transformed from the inside out by the work of God himself, and it is this future action of the Lord which Jeremiah announces in the oracle of the new covenant (31:31–34). Yahweh would forgive the people all their past sin (v. 34). Now all the years of disobedience and apostasy would be wiped out, as if they never happened. Yahweh would receive his people back into fellowship with himself, in a new covenant, containing new *tôrāh* commandments. But this new *tôrāh* would not be like that given at Sinai or that given in Deuteronomy. Now it would be an inner law, written upon the people's hearts, so that there would no longer be Deuteronomy's necessity to teach the commandments. Now everyone would know the commandments of God. The new *tôrāh* would be the inner guide and power and motivation of all conduct, so that every person could be obedient and love God, with all his heart and mind and strength (cf. Ezek. 11:17–20; 36:22–32; Ps. 51:10–12).

Such was the vision of the future Jeremiah saw as Jerusalem lay under siege, and such was the hope the prophet proclaimed as the walls of the city were breached and Judah's nationhood went up in flames. The word of God seems ever to be so—proclaiming that there is life though death be all around (cf. Luke 21:28), holding out the future of God when man's ways are at an end, heralding the triumph of a resurrection when only the defeat of a cross can be seen. Finally our salvation lies solely in the action of God: it was that message which Jeremiah preached, and indeed, which he lived.

The prophet, like Moses, never lived to enter into the fulfillment of the promise. Unlike Moses, he never even saw it from afar (cf. Deut. 34:1–4). But there was one fulfillment of the promise which Jeremiah did experience personally: God never forsook him. In the beginning of his ministry, he received the promise, "Be not afraid of them, for I am with you to deliver you" (1:8). When Jeremiah's faith was at the breaking point, that promise was renewed (15:20). Though his battle with his apostate people never came to an end, Jeremiah found that the Lord of hosts never left his side, and it was the presence of that dread Warrior and faithful Father which sustained the prophet to his death. In the supporting, demanding, unceasing faithfulness of God, the prophet too found his salvation.

When Jerusalem was taken, Jeremiah was treated well by the Babylonians and allowed to remain in his devastated country. (Apparently the order of the text is 38:28b; 39:3, 14, 11–13; 40:1–6; LXX omits 39:4–13). Judah was organized into the provincial system of the Babylonian Empire, and Gedaliah, who was the grandson of the reformer Shaphan and who had been chief minister in Zedekiah's cabinet, was appointed governor. Since Jerusalem was uninhabitable, the government was at Mizpah, eight miles to the north.

A man of wise and generous instincts, Gedaliah began the reconstruction of his ruined country (40:7–12), urging upon the people submission to Babylon "that it might be 'good' to them" (v. 9 Hebr.). We do not know how long his rule lasted—probably only a few months—but it was tragically ended by a group under the leadership of one Ishmael ben Nethaniah, who opposed the policy of collaboration (41:1–3). Wreaking havoc as they went, Ishmael's guerrillas slaughtered the officials at Mizpah and fled toward Ammon with a large group of hostages, among them Jeremiah (vv. 4–10; cf. 42:2). A company under the leadership of Johanan ben Kareah soon released the hostages, but Ishmael escaped to Ammon (vv. 11–16).

The question then was, how would Babylonia react to the murder of Gedaliah? Johanan and the people turned to Jeremiah to ask him whether or not they should flee to Egypt, and they promised that they would heed the prophet's word, that it might be "good" to them (42:1–6). After waiting ten days for revelation, Jeremiah received the word: the people should remain in Judah, where Yahweh would "build" them and "plant" them. They should not be afraid of the Babylonians, for now Yahweh was with them to deliver them: the Holy War would now be Yahweh's fight for his people (vv. 10–11).

As always, the people did not heed Jeremiah's word from God. They fled into Egypt, taking Baruch and Jeremiah with them (chap. 43). The last picture we have is of the prophet in Egypt, still proclaiming the word of God to a faithless and apostate people, still acting the spokesman of Yahweh's judgment on disobedience, still proclaiming that it was the word of God and not the word of men which would stand (chap. 44; cf. v. 28).

Jeremiah never saw the new covenant become reality. Like those heroes of faith in the Epistle to the Hebrews, he "did not receive what was promised, since God had foreseen something better for us, that apart from us" he should not be made perfect (Heb. 11:39f.). It remained for another Hebrew to fulfill Jeremiah's vision, and indeed, to complete his suffering: "This cup is the new covenant in my blood" (1 Cor. 11:25). In the crucifixion and resurrection of Jesus Christ, the new covenant became flesh. The promised forgiveness was given, and the Spirit was poured out, to write God's will upon our hearts and to give us the power of obedience (cf. 2 Cor. 3:3; 5:17; John 3:3, 5). In the final new Prophet like Moses (cf. Acts 3:22ff.), the story of Deuteronomy and Jeremiah found its completion. God's word did indeed stand. It will always stand.

# NOTES

1. William Neil, "Prophets of Israel: Jeremiah and Ezekiel," *Bible Guides,* vol. 8. ed. W. Barclay and F. F. Bruce (London: Lutterworth, and Nashville: Abingdon), p. 24.
2. William L. Holladay, "Background of Jeremiah's Self-understanding: Moses, Samuel, and Psalm 22," *Journal of Biblical Literature* 83 (1964): 161.

# SELECTED BIBLIOGRAPHY

## DEUTERONOMY

ACHTEMEIER, PAUL and ELIZABETH. *To Save all People: A Study of the Record of God's Redemptive Acts in Deuteronomy and Matthew.* Boston: United Church, 1967.

ALT, ALBRECHT. *Essays on Old Testament History and Religion.* Translated by R. A. Wilson. Oxford: Blackwell, 1966.

BÄCHLI, OTTO. *Israel und die Völker: Eine Studie zum Deuteronomium.* Abhandlungen zur Theologie des Alten und Neuen Testaments, vol. 41. Zürich: Zwingli Verlag, 1962.

BLAIR, EDWARD P. "An Appeal to Remembrance: The Memory Motif in Deuteronomy." *Interpretation* 15 (1961): 41–47.

BRIGHT, JOHN. *A History of Israel,* 2d ed. Philadelphia: Westminster, 1972.

BRUEGGEMANN, WALTER A. "The Kerygma of the Deuteronomistic Historian." *Interpretation* 22 (1968): 387–402.

90     SELECTED BIBLIOGRAPHY

CLEMENTS, RONALD E. *God's Chosen People: A Theological Interpretation of the Book of Deuteronomy*. London: SCM, 1968.
CRAIGIE, PETER C. *The Book of Deuteronomy*. New International Commentary on the Old Testament. Grand Rapids: Eerdmans, 1976.
DUMERMUTH, FRITZ. "Zur deuteronomischen Kulttheologie und ihren Voraussetzungen." *Zeitschrift für die alttestamentaliche Wissenschaft* 70 (1958): 59–98.
HYATT, J. PHILIP. "The Deuteronomic Edition of Jeremiah." *Vanderbilt Studies in the Humanities*, vol. 1. Nashville: Vanderbilt University, 1951.
KLINE, MEREDITH G. *Treaty of the Great King: The Covenant Structure of Deuteronomy*. Grand Rapids: Eerdmans, 1963.
LOHFINK, NORBERT. *Das Hauptgebot: Eine Untersuchung literarischer Einleitungsfragen zu Deuteronomium 5–11*. Rome: Pontifical Biblical Institute, 1963.
MCCARTHY, DENNIS J. *Treaty and Covenant: A Study in Form in the Ancient Oriental Documents and in the Old Testament*. Rome: Pontifical Biblical Institute, 1963.
MCCURLEY, FOSTER R., JR. "The Home of Deuteronomy Revisited: A Methodological Analysis of the Northern Theory." *A Light Unto My Path: Old Testament Studies in Honor of Jacob M. Myers*. Edited by H. Bream, R. Heim, C. Moore. Philadelphia: Temple University, 1974.
MENDENHALL, GEORGE. *Law and Covenant in Israel and the Ancient Near East*. Reprinted from *Biblical Archeologist* 17 (1954): 26–46, 49–76. Pittsburgh: The Biblical Colloquim, 1955.
MILLER, PATRICK D., JR. *The Divine Warrior in Early Israel*. Harvard Semitic Monograph, vol. 5. Cambridge: Harvard University, 1973.
_____ "The Gift of God: The Deuteronomic Theology of the Land." *Interpretation* 23 (1969): 451–465.
MORAN, WILLIAM L. "The Ancient Near Eastern Background of the Love of God in Deuteronomy." *Catholic Biblical Quarterly* 25 (1963): 77–87.
MYERS, JACOB M. "The Requisites for Response: On the Theology of Deuteronomy." *Interpretation* 15 (1961): 14–31.
NICHOLSON, ERNEST W. *Deuteronomy and Tradition*. Philadelphia: Fortress, 1967.
NOTH, MARTIN. "The Re-presentation of the Old Testament in Proclamation." *Essays on Old Testament Hermeneutics*. Edited by C. Westermann. Richmond: John Knox, 1963.
VON RAD, GERHARD. *Deuteronomy*. Philadelphia: Westminster, 1966.
_____ "Deuteronomy." *The Interpreter's Dictionary of the Bible*, vol. 1. Nashville: Abingdon, 1962.
_____ *Der Heilige Krieg in alten Israel*. Zürich: Zwingli-Verlag, 1961.
_____ *The Problem of the Hexateuch and Other Essays*. Edinburgh: Oliver and Boyd, 1965.
_____ *Studies in Deuteronomy*. London: SCM, 1953.
THOMPSON, JOHN A. *Deuteronomy: An Introduction and Commentary*. London: Inter-Varsity, 1974.
TOOMBS, LAWRENCE E. "Love and Justice in Deuteronomy: A Third Approach to the Law." *Interpretation* 19 (1965): 399–411.

DE TILIESSE, G. MINETTE. "Sections 'tu' et Sections 'vous' dans le Deutéronome." *Vetus Testamentum* 12 (1962): 29–87.
WEINFELD, MOSHE. *Deuteronomy and the Deuteronomic School.* Oxford: Clarendon, 1972.
WENHAM, GORDON J. "Deuteronomic Theology of the Book of Joshua." *Journal of Biblical Literature* 90 (1971): 140–148.
WRIGHT, G. ERNEST. "Introduction and Exegesis of Deuteronomy." *The Interpreter's Bible,* vol. 2. Nashville: Abingdon, 1953.


## JEREMIAH

BARDTKE, HANS. "Jeremia, der Fremdvölkerprophet." *Zeitschrift für die alttestamentliche Wissenschaft* 53 (1935). 209–239; 54 (1936): 240–262.
BERRIDGE, JOHN M. *Prophet, People and the Word of Yahweh.* Zürich: EVZ-Verlag, 1970.
BRIGHT, JOHN. *Jeremiah.* The Anchor Bible, vol. 21. New York: Doubleday, 1964.
CHILDS, BREVARD S. "The Enemy from the North and the Chaos Tradition." *Journal of Biblical Literature* 78 (1959): 187–198.
CORNILL, C. H. *Das Buch Jeremia.* Leipzig: B. Tauchnitz, 1905.
EISSFELDT, OTTO. "Jeremiah." *The Old Testament: An Introduction.* Translated by P. R. Ackroyd. New York: Harper and Row, 1965.
_____ "The Prophetic Literature." *The Old Testament and Modern Study.* Edited by H. H. Rowley. Oxford: Clarendon, 1951.
GOTTWALD, NORMAN K. *All the Kingdoms of the Earth: Israelite Prophecy and International Relations in the Ancient Near East.* New York: Harper and Row, 1964.
GORDON, THOMAS C. "A New Date for Jeremiah." *Expository Time* 44 (1932–33): 562–565.
HESCHEL, ABRAHAM J. *The Prophets.* New York: Harper and Row, 1962.
HOLLADAY, WILLIAM L. "Background of Jeremiah's Self-understanding: Moses, Samuel, and Psalm 22." *Journal of Biblical Literature* 83 (1964): 153–164.
_____ "The Covenant of the Patriarchs Overturned: Jeremiah's Intention in 'Terror on Every Side' (Jer. 20: 1–6)" *Journal of Biblical Literature* 91 (1972): 305–320.
_____ "Jeremiah's Lawsuit with God: A Study in Suffering and Meaning." *Interpretation* 17 (1963): 280–287.
_____ *Jeremiah: Spokesman Out of Time.* Philadelphia: United Church, 1974.
_____ "Prototype and Copies: A New Approach to the Poetry-Prose Problem in the Book of Jeremiah." *Journal of Biblical Literature* 79 (1960): 351–367.
_____ "The Recovery of Poetic Passages of Jeremiah." *Journal of Biblical Literature* 85 (1966): 401–435.
_____ "Style, Irony, and Authenticity in Jeremiah." *Journal of Biblical Literature* 81 (1962): 44–54.

HYATT, J. PHILIP. "Introduction and Exegesis of Jeremiah." *The Interpreter's Bible*, vol. 5. Nashville: Abingdon, 1956.

———— *Jeremiah, Prophet of Courage and Hope*. Nashville: Abingdon, 1958.

LESLIE, ELMER A. *Jeremiah*. Nashville: Abingdon, 1954.

LINDBLOM, JOHANNES. *Prophecy in Ancient Israel*. Philadelphia: Fortress, 1962.

MUILENBURG, JAMES. "Jeremiah the Prophet." *The Interpreter's Dictionary of the Bible*, vol. 2. Nashville: Abingdon, 1962.

MOWINCKEL, SIGMUND. *Zur Komposition des Buches Jeremia*. Kristiania (Oslo): in Kommission bei Jacob Dybwad, 1914.

NEIL, WILLIAM. *Prophets of Israel: Jeremiah and Ezekiel*. Vol. 8. Bible Guides. Edited by W. Barclay and F. F. Bruce. Published jointly in London: Lutterworth; Nashville: Abingdon, 1961–1965.

NICHOLSON, ERNEST W. *The Book of the Prophet Jeremiah; Chapters 1–25, 26–52*. Cambridge Bible Commentary. Cambridge: University, 1973, 1975.

VON RAD, GERHARD. *Old Testament Theology*. 2 vols. Translated by D. M. G. Stalker. Edinburgh and London: Oliver and Boyd, 1962, 1965.

ROBINSON, T. H. "Baruch's Roll." *Zeitschrift für die alttestamentliche Wissenschaft* 42 (1924): 209–221.

ROWLEY, HAROLD H. "The Prophet Jeremiah and the Book of Deuteronomy." *Studies in Old Testament Prophecy*. New York: Scribner's, 1950.

RUDOLPH, WILHELM. *Jeremia*. Handbuch zum Alten Testament. Tübingen: J. C. B. Mohr, 1947.

SKINNER, JOHN. *Prophecy and Religion: Studies in the Life of Jeremiah*. Cambridge: University, 1940.

SMITH, GEORGE A. *Jeremiah*. 4th ed. New York: Harper, 1929.

WEIPPERT, HELGA. "Die Prosareden des Jeremiasbuches." Beiheft zur *Zeitschrift für die alttestamentliche Wissenschaft*, 132. Berlin: de Gruyter, 1973.

WELCH, ADAM C. *Jeremiah, His Time and Work*. London: Oxford University, 1928.

# INDEX OF BIBLICAL PASSAGES

93